D.I.E.T.
(DID I EAT THAT?)

THE FINDING OF MYSELF
THE LOSING OF 135 POUNDS

JUDY MINNIS COWART
WITH INTRODUCTION BY FRED REIFSTECK, M.D.

D.I.E.T.
(Did I Eat That?)
The Finding of Myself
The Losing of 135 Pounds

ISBN #0-9644073-0-2

If unavailable in local bookstores, additional copies of this book may be purchased by writing to the author at:

THE NEXT CHAPTER
Post Office Box 355
Jonesboro, Georgia 30237

A CC PRODUCTION
First Edition, 1995

Distributed by Southern Publishers Group • 800/628-0903

Daddy and Barbara
Sunday afternoon in the park
Spring of 1941

To the Glory of God

To the Memory of
my daddy
JAMES WESLEY MINNIS
1903–1975
and
my sister
BARBARA MINNIS MORRIS
1937 – 1990

In Honor of
JACK FRANKLIN MORRIS
who valiantly stood with his wife
as he gently knelt by her side

With love and appreciation to those on whom I leaned until I could stand alone

WILLIAM JOHN COWART
the man who stands beside me
the man I am blessed to call my husband

THE REVEREND C. NEWELL ANDERSON
my priest and my friend
whose guidance and direction led me to acceptance and peace

A MAN I CALL BILL
his spirit touched me with hope
by his presence and influence I came a great distance

To the Absolute Pride and Joy of My Life
KIRBY WADE COWART
KEVIN HOWELL COWART
honesty, dependability, frivolity and laughter
sons in whom we are well pleased

and most especially
to my mother and sisters
with love and hope

With special recognition and heartfelt thanks, I acknowledge invaluable contributions from others who traveled this journey with me

CAROLYN TUZUNER, my mentor, counselor, companion, angel and loving friend, who believed in me, opened an important door for me, then cared enough to hold my hand and walk with me into that room in my life

KEITH HUFFSTETTER, EARL AND EDITH HUNTER, who, with unselfish caring and understanding, became bridges over troubled waters

JONELLE GARRETT, JEAN GIBSON, JEANNE CONDREY RUST, the other three of The Four-J's; dear friends who are true gifts from God

NEWELL, TISA, JONATHAN, CHRISTINA, who graciously and lovingly allowed me to interrupt their home life as *I burned the midday and midnight oil* at their computer

DAVID REES PALMER, a guardian angel who sat with me, opened a door to a room which I didn't know was there, and thus contributed to my peace

PEPPER MACKINNON, who listened and supported, never judging, while gently holding me with understanding

DIANE HARDEN, YVONNE JONES, GERRY WOODLE, for always being my cheerleaders

ARTHUR DEBAISE, a cherished friend, an endearing smile

BOB BARNARD, BETTY JO MORRIS, MARIE SCHNELLE, *the adoption committee* that made Delta Air Lines possible for me

BRYCE BEYLER (the very polite young man at Walmart!) who bailed me out and kept me from drowning in the unknown of a new computer system

JANETTE HILL, who has traveled with me mile after mile, stuck with me thru thick and thin and high and low, while sharing both my tears and laughter

With smiles and warmth to my DELTA AIR LINES and ST. JOHN'S PARISH FAMILIES, whose love and support are always with me

And in tribute to some very special people in my life who have, with courage, personally faced cancer: Kim Alvis, Ginger Edwards, Linda Eickhoff, Elam Gillon, D.R. Harris, Fred Hightower, Christina Palmer, Joan Schneider, Dorothy Scribner, Renee Vaughn, and Alfred Weeks

CONTENTS

FOREWORD

Daddy died in 1975 without causing too much stir. I loved him, mourned his death and the loss of him from my life. Sadly, he died at Christmas time and it was many years before I could again fully enjoy the celebration of this glorious season without the shadow of the memory of his death. But even with these annual reminders, his death was tolerable. After all, parents are supposed to get old and die; and this was just the natural flow of life as far as I was concerned.

But the death of a sister wasn't expected. Barbara was diagnosed as having Burkitt's lymphoma, a form of cancer, in September of 1989. A few days later, at her fifty-second birthday, she received the first of numerous chemotherapy treatments. She courageously struggled through a hard battle, but finally lost in her fight for life.

Eight months later, on May 28, 1990, Barbara was buried. Her death was the beginning of a rebirth for me, a search I began in my struggle to survive.

While this is my story, it is Barbara's story, too; for through her death I found myself and more happiness and contentment than I could ever have dreamed possible.

Perhaps it is true that something good does come from everything, but why did I have to lose my beloved sister to find my own peace?

INTRODUCTION

FRED REIFSTECK, M.D.

Much is written about weight loss and dieting. As a medical doctor, I see numerous patients who have serious health problems resulting from obesity, and either they do not understand or do not realize that their excess weight is contributing to physical and emotional problems.

Various weight loss programs have been developed; some are healthy, some are not. The unhealthy approaches can be dangerous and should be avoided. The problem is that many people do not *understand* that the *programs* and *diets* are unhealthy. It is promising to review weight loss information that is healthy and offers more than just following a diet.

This book is more than an account of a diet and the struggle to lose weight. It is an examination of the author's life, including both high and low emotional points. Judy takes an introspective look at herself in order to determine how she arrived at the point that she said, "I must lose weight." This was not easy, and was much more than just saying the words. Most people don't accept the importance and necessity of this and in the long run are unsuccessful at weight loss.

Judy tore down many perceptions, both internally and externally formed, that had kept her from taking the steps necessary to successfully lose weight. The willingness to relate her difficult journey should serve as an inspiration to the reader.

The struggle to lose weight is more than diet or exercise. It is a lifestyle change which one must start by examining self-image and self-esteem. The habits started in childhood may become firmly established, and thus difficult to change; but successful weight loss can never be accomplished without starting at this fundamental point. Everyone will not enter the same depth of introspection that Judy did, but each must be willing to do some examination.

I see many patients who wish to lose weight and are ultimately unsuccessful and I feel the primary reason for this is that they are not willing to undertake the self examination process. Perhaps these people can gain strength by reading this book. This book in itself will not make the personal task easier, but it will serve as a reminder that it can be done.

Weight reduction may very well be one of the most difficult life changes undertaken. Judy's story proves this point and at the same time confirms that it is possible.

The battle only begins with weight reduction. Once successful, one will have to continue the hard work to keep off the lost weight. To maintain the weight loss, the lessons learned along the way must be applied daily. The benefits of keeping the weight off affect both physical and mental well being.

As you read this book, recognize and understand the message, then formulate and execute a plan for yourself, you'll hopefully arrive at the same destination as Judy. Like her, you may reach a level of celebration and realization that the battle can be won.

How queer everything is today! And yesterday things went on just as usual. I wonder if I've been changed in the night? Let me think: was I the same when I got up this morning? I almost think I can remember feeling a little different. But if I'm not the same, the next question is, "Who in the world am I?" Ah, that's the great puzzle!

A l i c e   i n   W o n d e r l a n d
by: Lewis Carroll

PART ONE

REALITY

NEVER QUIT TRYING

*T*his is about a look inside myself which I refer to as my journey, my soul-searching of more than five years' duration, my fight for survival. The outward and visible sign of the inward and invisible changes in my life is the loss of 135 pounds of excess body weight. I'll take that gain (or loss, as you may want to call it) in my life any day and be thrilled with it, but this weight loss was only a bonus to what else I discovered.

At one point during this journey, when I dropped more than twenty pounds in body weight with no conscious effort on my part, I realized something special was happening in my life so I began to look closer at what was going on. In order to shed additional pounds, I performed a tedious task which resulted in giving up my baggage of guilt and wings of perfection and letting go of trying to control life. Once I managed to arrive at that destination I finally found the real me and no longer had to feed the guilt in my life. The excess weight I was carrying simply seemed to fall off.

I am neither a nutritionist nor a dietician, nor would I dare to presume to set out a menu plan for anyone else. There are many good weight loss diets available which will work when one is ready to fully commit to facing and changing obsessive behavior. Simply wanting to change the behavior isn't good enough. First there must be motivation, an unshakable reason to accomplish change, motivation to hang onto when all else fails. That reason has to be greater than anything else. If you're wanting to make a change in your life, find your motivation and be ready to hold to this as if you were lost at sea and clinging to a capsized boat. Success depends on keeping that motivation in front of you. Don't ever forget that.

You may already know your motivation; you may find it today, tomorrow, next week, next month, or even next year. Keep looking, and when you find it, hang on. Remember, we never fail until we quit trying.

When I was seven months pregnant with my second child I saw an anti-smoking campaign commercial on television which was sponsored by the American Cancer Society. I had been smoking for several years and had never consciously given any thought to quitting. But when I saw that commercial I realized there was a reason for me to quit smoking, and that reason was my unborn child and my year old son. I did not want my children to smoke because of the health dangers it presented. My children became my motivation. At that very instant I put down that pack of cigarettes and ended my smoking. Cold turkey. Done. Finished. I now detest the very odor of cigarettes as well as the smoke from them, but at that time I even enjoyed smelling smoke from others cigarettes. That's not to say that I was never again tempted to smoke. For years after quitting, while I slept I even dreamed of smoking. Yes, I wanted another cigarette, but not nearly as much as I wanted my children not to smoke. I knew that children learn what they live and I chose to set the example of not smoking rather than the other way around.

That is what I mean by motivation! I never wanted a cigarette as much as I wanted good health for my sons.

A Time of Crisis

During a period of approximately four years I experienced several major events in my life in rapid succession, some more severe than others, but each of which took a tremendous toll of me, both physically and emotionally. As always in the past, I thought I was doing exceptionally well with every event; taking control, handling efficiently and sufficiently as needed. When I had any one at a point where I could let go of it for a while, I would place the residual remains *on the shelf* in my life; each always in the back of my mind as not yet quite finished, labeled *HANDLE WITH CARE—DO NOT DISTURB—TO BE HANDLED AS TIME PERMITS*.

My shelf gathered unfinished business continually. As it grew heavier and heavier, there was a tilt and sag which became more pronounced with each addition; and the fastenings slowly, surely, and constantly stretched and strained under the weight it was holding.

7

The beginning of the collapse of my shelf came in the Fall of 1988 with the ringing of the telephone as I stood in the kitchen at home, getting things squared away from the evening meal we had just completed. With two teenage sons, one puppy, three cats, one television and two radios all functioning near maximum level in our household, it certainly was not in the quiet of the night. The call was from one of my four sisters regarding our youngest sister. This sister, with whom I had not had enough contact in recent years simply because I was into the habit of being too busy to maintain and enjoy close personal relationships, had reached a crisis point in her life and it was now time to become involved in helping her. Personal relationships, like neglected flowers, suffer from lack of attention. However, one good thing about family is that love and relationships can be renewed.

With this phone call I automatically assumed responsibility to take care of this situation as always in the past, with no question nor thought of refusal.

Thus began the series of events which ultimately brought about a drastic change in my life.

For several years this sister had been under the care of a physician who had prescribed medication for her without proper monitoring of its effects. Over a period of time she had become excessively medicated from these drugs and was having severe adverse reactions. It was now time to bind together as a family unit to help her. Sadly, as this sister had been going through her own time of emotional upheaval, I was unaware of anything she was experiencing. Once the crisis stage was reached, though, I was brought into the situation and immediately had to take control to get her the help she needed; no matter that there were others who should have also participated in helping. I didn't have time for that, I had to do it all and do it now.

Linda was finally hospitalized; and, with her in the care of competent professionals, I could get on to the next event. I had taken care of this the best that I could, even though it was not to my satisfaction. When I could let go, with a sigh of relief I added this unfinished business to my already over-loaded shelf.

Next came unemployment for my husband. Within two weeks of twenty-five years of service with a major retail de-partment store he, along with several thousand other employ-ees nationwide, was terminated from his job. While this was not unexpected, it took its toll. We had recently purchased our dream home at the lake, with a very large increase in monthly mortgage payments. That shouldn't be a problem, we naively thought; after all, we were hard-working people who had never had any problems with financial responsibili-ties and everything would be alright. That turned out to be not necessarily correct.

The one thing we weren't expecting nor prepared for was the months of unemployment continuing as my husband found the difficulty of competing with the younger genera-tion for the available jobs and finding out how unmarketable he was as a forty-nine-year-old man with limited experience beyond the one company with whom he had been associ-ated since his discharge from the army.

We continually dipped into the savings and profit-shar-ing to supplement the unemployment checks, until this was depleted. Thank God for unselfish friends and family with-out whom we would never have survived financially.

Nearly a year later he found employment: two full-time jobs to almost equal the income of the position vacated.

These leftovers were now shelved; and, with this addi-tion, the sag of my shelf became even more pronounced.

Events didn't necessarily stand in line and wait until the previous ones were completed and filed away. Oh, no! That would have made life just a little less realistic. Most of the time they overlapped so I was never free from one before going into the next. It was rather like weaving a rug, the strings pulling in separate directions, taunt and tight, back and forth. Pressure! Pressure! Pressure! And the movement seemed continuous, with each crisis simply adding more material to the complexity.

So it was the third time. Without warning, with number two still underway, this one came on the scene and stayed around to continue into the fourth.

Time now for my mother to have her problems, which were almost identical to those my sister had just experienced. The fact that this was the second time around meant only that I could list *experienced* on this form, for it didn't make handling this one a bit easier than any of the others. In fact, there was only my husband to assist as the other sisters would not be involved this time. That didn't matter, though, because, as usual, I could be in control and handle this one, too.

It was mother this time who was over-medicated by the same physician who had also been treating my sister; and she, too, had her adverse reaction to the prescription drugs she was taking.

When mother's condition reached the critical point, she was visiting with my sister, Barbara, at her home located about fifty miles from our residence. When mother obviously had to have professional intercession, Barbara called and told me of the situation, unplugged her telephone, left mother alone in the house and went off to work.

I accepted the responsibility without any thought of doing otherwise, assuming the role of leadership once again for my family, and began immediately to take care of this one, too. Of course I could handle this situation which lasted only several months and took no more than the remainder of my available waking hours. All I had to do this time was to get mother hospitalized for necessary medical treatment and maintain daily contact with her by visiting during this hospitalization while arranging housing and furnishings for her to have upon discharge from the hospital. So we got through that one. Time to file away number three and get on to the next requirement of me by this thing called life.

Did I just imagine that, or did my shelf again seem to tip downward with this additional weight?

Shortly after my mother's hospitalization, the doctor who had been treating and prescribing medication for both my sister and my mother was admitted to a drug rehabilitation program for treatment of drug addiction. I have since been advised by experts in that field that this doctor had exhibited a classic symptom of drug abuse in the medical profession in that he was indiscriminately prescribing controlled drugs for his patients. How sad that he lost his medical practice and years later continued to undergo treatment himself in a drug rehabilitation program.

Okay, ready or not, right in the middle of number three, here comes the fourth event for my attention.

At the age of six, our firstborn son, Kirby, was found to be hearing impaired and additional testing revealed extensive learning disabilities; but this son didn't let any of this ever discourage him in life. He had a dream of becoming a Marine and he wasn't going to be stopped. He even went to summer school during his high school years so as to be able to get his diploma early, and entered the U. S. Marine Corps in March of 1989.

Less than twenty-four hours after arriving for basic training at Parris Island, South Carolina, a physical examination exposed the hearing loss, and he was disillusioned with the reality of the situation. His first letter home stated, "I've got good news and bad news. The good news is I'm not going to stay. The bad news is I'll be here at least a full month." It didn't take many hours in this atmosphere for him to decide that this career choice wasn't as he had anticipated it would be.

This was a month of contact possible only through letters, when personal contact was longed for so much and was one time any and all control was denied me. I felt totally helpless. Contact could, of course, be maintained through letters, but that just wasn't sufficient when my child was away from home and on his own for the first time in life. Our priest was able to be in contact with the chaplain at Parris Island and this, while not what I would have chosen, did give us more information about the well-being of Kirby than could be accomplished through letters.

A few weeks later Kirby returned home, already making plans for further education. With a keen interest in food preparation, he was going to follow his second career choice to become a chef. Kirby made application and was accepted to begin the Fall quarter at a school in Rhode Island, and was also offered an opportunity to participate in their summer work program. Taking part in this program would give him experience in this career, provide regular income and make him eligible for partial payment of tuition. Does that sound too good to be true? It was!

Kirby left for school late in June, and less than two weeks into the summer employment he fell and severely damaged his knee. Emergency treatment was given and the phone call came that Kirby was going to have to come home for medical care. There he was, more than a thousand miles from home. Take it one step at a time! Wire an airline ticket to Providence and get him home. Of course, this was quite an unexpected and unplanned expense. Next, deal with lengthy and extensive medical care and be chauffeur for daily physical therapy. Get him back on his feet and well enough to return to school in time for the beginning of the quarter, only to have him again injure the knee within three weeks. Here we go again. Get him back home, into more extensive medical treatment, finally surgery followed by more physical therapy, then find out that the workers' compensation insurance refuses to pay for the medical expenses incurred. That meant I could now help my son locate an attorney in the Boston area to handle this one more problem in which we would be involved for several months even after medical treatment was complete. The ultimate outcome of this injury was that Kirby could no longer pursue this career choice.

By now, it's obvious son number one is going to be closer to home for schooling for a while. Take a deep breath, and crisis number four goes to the shelf. And my shelf again dips downward.

Am I overwhelmed yet? tired? ready to throw in the towel? Of course not. Why should I be? I'm in control. I'm capable. I can deal with it all. No problem! Keep going, everything's going to be okay. Remember that I'm an optimistic person, that it's all in the attitude. I'm doing just fine. There will be time tomorrow for what's left over from today. Haven't I said for years that when I die I don't want there to be any leftovers in my life, that I want all my gifts to be used up? See, I'm doing fine. I'm happy. I'm coping. I'm managing. I have to do it, and I can!

Ready or not, here it comes. Even before the previous remains are shelved, I see crisis number five on the horizon.

Like many women today, my sister Barbara dreamed of owning and operating her own business. However, during the busy time of preparation and opening of this venture she had unexplained pain in her legs for which the medical profession could find no diagnosis. Finally a C.T. scan was performed and a tumor was found in the her upper back area. Barbara was scheduled for outpatient surgery with the intent to return to work within a couple of days. She never returned to her work again. Biopsy of the tumor revealed malignant Burkitt's lymphoma. Extensive and radical treatment was begun within a matter of days, with untold days and nights of hospitalization required.

While all of this was taking place, I was working three part-time jobs. This allowed me the flexibility I wanted for myself while also providing a reasonable income. However, time had come for me to get back to a full-time occupation for income and at the same time I felt I needed to begin looking seriously towards preparation for future retirement. Before marriage, I had worked in an office with the government and was able to return there in a clerical position. Even though I had to once again begin in an entry-level position, I could look forward to picking up my previous nine years of service towards retirement upon completion of an additional two years of employment.

Now it's time. Crisis number six, stand and be recognized.

And number six threw me into a panic.

From the moment I had met my husband-to-be twenty-four years earlier, I never knew another man existed. Ours had been a storybook romance from that moment forward. He was my prince charming and we were living happily ever after. Without warning, the perfection cracked.

Within weeks in this new job I was totally infatuated with this boss, this wonderful man the likes of which I had never known before. But I couldn't do that! How could this happen to me! I tried to ignore the feelings and pretend they didn't exist, but that only worked for a while until complications happened.

About three months after I was hired the boss left his position for other employment. When he told me of his plans and that he would be leaving the next day, I took this news with mixed emotions. I was happy for him while I also knew I was going to miss him terribly. The following day, which was our final time together at the office, I remarked to him just hours before he left that I felt *as if someone had died*.

Ten days later my sister lost her fight with cancer.

The plan of treatment for Barbara had been for a bone marrow transplant to be accomplished when the cancer was in remission. Almost three months into treatment, shortly before Christmas, Barbara was in remission and was sent home to rest and regain her strength in preparation for the extensive treatment required for this procedure. Before the bone marrow could be harvested the cancer reoccurred. Efforts were again put forth through extensive chemotherapy treatments for a second remission. Ten days prior to her death the treating physicians pronounced her *about 90 percent clear*, and a massive dose of chemotherapy was administered with intent to harvest the bone marrow immediately upon accomplishment of the remission.

Two days later Barbara was told that the cancer had won, that it had taken over and nothing further could be done to stop it. She waited for her treating physician to return to the hospital; when he confirmed to her that no further treatment would be effective, Barbara turned over in the bed to face the wall in that hospital room. Five days later she accepted death.

Then crisis number seven arrived and nearly destroyed me. Now came the unavoidable complications.

The night following my sister's death I experienced a nightmare that was horrible beyond my comprehension. The next night that same haunting nightmare returned, only to be followed by a second nightmare just as unbearable. With both, I was awakened by the sound of my own screaming. Every time I drifted off to sleep one or both of the nightmares would repeat. To avoid the nightmares, I desperately fought sleep and just catnapped off and on for more than a year.

But the human body cannot maintain itself without adequate rest, and I was discovering this firsthand. I developed extreme physical pain from the lack of sleep. No matter how hard I fought, though, there were times that I couldn't hold on and I would unavoidably slip into sleep and always there would be those monster nightmares waiting for me.

This, then, was the beginning of my journey, my search for survival.

15

I couldn't even begin to put away crises numbers five or six or seven, or any others thereafter. That shelf, where I had stored the shabbily organized world which I had created through control, silently tore lose and soundlessly but tragically crashed down on my life and in my heart. All that had been there now covered me.

Things were happening in my life about which I could do absolutely nothing. I was smothered, completely out of control. I felt as if an oversized fisherman's knife with its sharp, pointed blade and serrated edges, held by two giant hands, had with one slow, continuous, deliberate motion, ripped open my soul from top to bottom, and the exposed pain was unbelievably raw and intense.

If I were going to survive, I would have to dig out, reassess, sort, and throw away. I didn't specifically realize that just then; I only knew that I had to find the cause of this pain and make it go away. My life was as a broken shell and I couldn't expect to glue it back together. No paint and wallpaper job, this one. This was going to require major reconstruction. I didn't know the impact of the healing process which lay ahead of me. There was a long and difficult path ahead which I would have to travel before I could get through the rapids to reach peaceful waters. I had always looked upon myself as a rock; now I found I was rather as a feather being cast about by the wind, as it falls from a bird in flight.

But I wasn't finished yet. No, not yet! There was still much more to face before I would ever find my peace.

Look. There it is, straight ahead, just on the horizon; it's happening again. One more unexpected event to face.

Our younger son, the honor student who was now in his senior year of high school, had the opportunity to attend college on the choice of either a full academic or football scholarship but had decided after fifteen of his eighteen years in attending classes that he was tired of school and was ready *to get on with his life*.

Unknown to his parents, he skipped school one day in early April, drove almost two hundred miles to Camp Mikell, a program of the Episcopal Diocese of Atlanta where he had enjoyed many happy camping sessions in years past, and spent the day there deciding his future. He came home that evening, told us what he had done and also what he had decided. He was going to follow in his brother's footsteps and become a Marine. Here we go again! The next day he went to the Marine Recruiting Station and signed up on a delayed entry program, to arrange to take his oath and leave for Parris Island in June. With high school graduation less than ten weeks away, he quit school, took tests for both his Georgia and Adult Equivalency Diplomas and shipped out to basic training as scheduled.

His first letter home was quite different from the one his brother had sent the year before. His was a question, "When do the real D.I.'s get here?" (He later reported that they had, in fact, finally shown up. No doubt about it!) He was in the final phase of basic training when the troop buildup began in the Persian Gulf, and was ready and waiting to go to war. But that wasn't to be. Instead of going to the land of sand, he was sent to Memphis, Tennessee, for more instructional training.

Isn't it interesting that he had become a Marine to avoid school, yet had chosen a Military Occupation Specialty (MOS) which required that he would be sent for further classroom education after basic training.

And life was hell for a trained killer who couldn't get to the war! In fact, to quote him, "Every generation has its war, and I missed mine."

In the meantime, back to my little corner of the world. For several weeks after the boss had left our office there was no work for me to do and, with no replacement yet on board in his place, I was just reporting to work each day to either do my own personal volunteer paperwork or nothing at all.

Seeing that this was going nowhere fast, and knowing I had been left behind for the most part in preparation of skills

William, Judy, Kirby, Kevin
September of 1990

for today's job market, I decided to also resign my position and enroll in school for further training which would enable me to secure better employment. I followed through on this decision and began classes soon thereafter, once again returning to part-time work.

I was functioning on a daily basis but was no longer controlling crises for anyone, myself included.

Even though I was having incredible trouble now just trying to take care of my own life I was, without any knowledge that it was happening, establishing not only a pattern of survival but also beginning what I later discovered is a most important part of successful living. I was now learning to truly live one day at a time, which was all I had ever needed to do.

I had never before acknowledged any difficulty controlling my life and I had always managed to handle things up to a point that I could put them on my shelf in a somewhat acceptable manner. No longer could I do that, for now my shelf had collapsed and left me without even this false security upon which I had always relied.

I sure couldn't sleep, for those all consuming nightmares were constantly hovering on the edge.

I was performing my job functions, attending classes daily, and putting forth a happy face, just trying to cope with my own life.

No one outside myself other than my husband, my priest, and one very special friend was aware of the silent turmoil bubbling within me; and even they didn't know the depth of my pain.

Both physical and emotional exhaustion tethered on the brink and I knew, without doubt, that I was going downhill. I was desperately trying to put on the brakes; God knows how I was trying. But trying was all I was doing. There was no doubt that I was in turmoil and on the precipice of emotional disaster.

My struggle for survival was now well underway.

THE DOOR OPENS

*T*he loss of my sister through death coupled with the separation from this man to whom I was attracted, no matter the denial, was more than I expected and I did not want to have to deal with it.

I was surrounded by people and movement and life, but I felt as if my voice were crying aloud in isolation, so alone in all this bustle and clamor of life.

I didn't want to cope anymore. Not anymore. The fight was gone this time and now I just wanted to retreat. But beyond that desire to hide away, I also knew that I wanted to survive and to enjoy life again.

In my continued storybook existence in my marriage I had always before been able to run to my husband anytime anything went wrong, he would put his arms around me and make the hurt go away, and everything would be alright. Even before that I had always had my mother. Not this time. Oh, no! Not this time. How could I go to my husband for comfort, to this man I had loved for so many years of my life, and tell him I was attracted to another man. And there was no way even he could make my sister not be dead.

For the first time in my life I was slapped in the face with reality. I knew I had to do something if I were going to survive. And in desperation I absolutely knew that I did want to survive, that life was precious to me and I wanted to be involved in it to the fullest extent.

Little did I know that beneath this pain was happiness which would erupt into my life at the end of this search beyond anything I had ever dreamed or experienced.

Before I could have this incredible happiness, though, I was going to have to learn to stand on my own two feet and realistically face life all by myself.

The package I was holding labeled *infatuation* became heavier and heavier. I was constantly attempting to push it away from my consciousness, but with no shelf to put it on I was lost. Finally, I tenderly began to glance around the edges.

I didn't know which way to turn.

One weekday afternoon when I was at our parish church for no special reason, I met my priest in the hallway and we spoke of the recent death of my sister. Continuing the conversation, we graduated to the rocking chairs in his office. We discussed life and death. We explored burial and cremation. I talked. I cried. And in anguish I told him of my terror of the unexpected cremation of my sister and of the horror and pain of her death which was tearing my soul to shreds.

Then, I unwillingly confessed to him about this other man.

Once this window in my heart was opened, it all poured forth: the pain, the infatuation, the feelings, the desires, the guilt. Then I was totally astounded when he told me I had to see this through or spend the remainder of my life wondering what would have happened if I didn't do so. He also pointed out to me that in doing this I had to keep in mind some possibilities which I absolutely did not want to hear nor face about what the outcome could be.

I continued to try to deny what I felt, but this denial wouldn't work! Rather than forgetting this man as I so desperately wanted to do, the feelings only continued; and, through his absence, increased. I found that out sight isn't necessarily out of mind. But, at least, I did keep seeking answers.

I knew without doubt that if I were going to survive I had to do something. This would require that I take a long and hard look at my life to find out what was important to me and the direction I would now be traveling. My life was turned topsy-turvy.

Father Anderson required of me that I tell my husband of what I was going through, but I could not do that. Sure, I was already sharing with him the pain and effects of my sister's death upon my life, but I wasn't yet ready to go to him about this other man. Not yet. Not until I could turn loose of it all, and I wasn't yet sure I wanted to even let go of these feelings.

My priest also pointed out to me that I had to keep in mind that divorce was a possible outcome of this situation, and that scared me even more than having this attraction to another man. Never had I ever considered that the option of divorce existed in my marriage. My husband and I had married each other with the intent of staying together in a happy marriage *'til death do us part* and I didn't see the prospect of this ever changing. Once, in a discussion with some friends, we were all talking about marriage and how many years each of the couples there had been married. Ours was of the shortest duration with us having recently celebrated our eighteenth anniversary. We were all feeling very proud of ourselves and our obvious successful unions, when my husband stated, "Ours has been very good so far, and if we're still together until one of us dies, then you can all know it was a successful marriage."

I have now come from behind my screen of naivety and see that everything we do in life is an option, and there is always an alternate choice for each and every decision we make and every action we take.

My priest was giving me good guidance and direction and advice, but that's not what I was hearing. My interpretation was, "Get a divorce, and go for it."

I was more confused than ever.

Many months later I finally looked at this sensibly and correctly realized that I didn't have to exercise that choice just because the option was there.

Oh, how much trouble we get into by not listening. Life is a little bit less confusing if we will only learn to listen. If in doubt, ask; but, for heaven's sake, don't go off half cocked.

Because I wasn't listening to what my priest said but only to what I thought he said, I knew there was no way I was going to follow his guidelines. Not when he wasn't telling me what I wanted to hear.

I wanted him to tell me to stay away from the temptation, to tell me what a good girl I was because I had done nothing to encourage the situation, and to give me all the answers in the standard replies so I could piously feel good about myself, and then for everything to be okay.

As usual, I wanted to pull the covers of life over my head and hide.

But he didn't make it so simple for me; and, thank God, he didn't. His guidance and direction required I use my mind and my heart and my soul and find my own answers. How much easier it would have been for me if I had only realized the sensibility of this and applied it right then and there instead of fighting so strongly just because it wasn't what I wanted to hear.

Having to personally seek my peace and go through the pain and fear and frustrations I experienced in this search and then to finally arrive at the joy and happiness I found expanded my world beyond any measure I could have ever imagined possible, and the personal growth I experienced was phenomenal.

More than a year passed before I saw this man again. A year filled with loss of sleep and pain and nightmares and frustration and unanswered questions. We met one afternoon for a couple of hours to share lunch while we again visited for a while, and thus finally began the acceptance and peace in this journey. I obviously had to see him again to go forward. That night there were no nightmares, only sweet sleep and a beautiful dream about my sister.

I deceived myself into believing this was finally the letting go of Barbara.

C HAPTER 3

PART TWO

YESTERDAY

PERFECTION IN ITSELF

Where is my copy of the instruction book for life?

All my life I've been an optimistic and happy person. I've been responsible, upstanding, agreeable, and done okay for the most part. I'm not an overly ambitious person nor do I have a desire for untold worldly possessions. I'm convinced that people are to be loved and things are to be enjoyed, and have lived true to that belief. I've been a contributing member to society and I get along with others without too much complaint. Yet, in spite of all this contentedness and still unknown to me, I was only skimming the surface of life.

The one shortcoming I had the most trouble with for years and years is that no matter how hard I tried, somehow I always managed to come up short on achieving perfection.

There was no doubt in my mind that perfection was required of me and no less than that was acceptable. Every hat on my head had to cover perfection. That meant I had to be perfect in every role in my life: as daughter, sister, student,

29

employee, date, bride, friend, wife, mother, volunteer, Christian, neighbor, and housekeeper. In every role, in everything I did in life, I had to be perfect. Nothing else would do.

The route to perfection may be somewhat vague, but it can be found in subtle ways.

First, I had to be ever aware of what everyone around me was doing, because I positively knew they were doing everything perfectly and I could absorb much information from them. Proof of this was that if I were as perfect as each of them would they not be criticizing me for my shortcomings.

Like the cat and mouse, I had to constantly watch and wait and then take the knowledge and information I would secretly find and file it away in my mind so that I, too, could achieve this state of perfection.

There was always the hope within me that I had what it took to achieve perfection; that perhaps I, too, would make it someday if I just kept striving.

THE PERFECT DAUGHTER

*A*nnalee, daughter of Levi Marion and Sarah Susannah Howell. Names which reflect and sound of a genteel time. My mother, Annalee, who was born shortly after the turn of the century in another state, where she was exposed to the rich plantation life. She knew of governesses and maids and butlers when she married and moved with her husband to Atlanta.

While their lifestyle changed with this relocation to the city, there was still the Old South tradition and culture in her and this very much influenced how we were raised. We were taught music and sewing and all the finer things that young ladies were expected to have in their repertoire.

Then, here I was, born at the beginning of World War II, a time which changed women's place in the world when the men went to war, when American women were catapulted from being housewives and homemakers into the workplace.

And to enhance that I was a teenager in the 1950's, which is widely recognized as the last years of innocence.

To say the least, I was caught in a time warp; and the Old South and this new culture beyond the '50s clashed in me, which resulted in my being wrong about everything.

When I was six years of age we moved from the city to the country, which is an area now just considered the suburbs. During those years it was difficult to distinguish between city and country other than by the difference in the spacing of the houses, the occasional presence of outhouses in the country, and the country roads were not always paved as were those in the city. At least in the country, though, we didn't have to dodge or bump over the trolley tracks as did the automobiles on the city streets.

With the changes that occurred in the city in the years following our move, I am so glad that I had the opportunity to live and grow up in a country environment. We had home grown vegetables from our garden, pastures to roam, woods in which to find muscadines and our own Christmas trees, creeks for wading, chickens to raise, numerous dogs and cats to cherish, and a mule to chase.

That mule, named Daisy, knew every way possible to get beyond the fences which were there for her restraint and she always managed to be out to do her own chasing of the occasional cars which passed our house. That in itself was another experience. The mule would go about five miles to a gas station where she would quietly stand and wait until I arrived, on foot, to walk back home with her. Of course, she wasn't about to be agreeable to allowing me to ride on her back as we returned home, but she never balked in quietly and humbly, with head appropriately cast downward, following me back down the road she had just traveled.

And what better experience for me to learn nurturing than by drying and warming baby chicks as they hatched on a wet spring day.

Growing up in the forties and fifties was totally unlike today. Those were different days and there were different rules. We didn't say what we thought; in fact, I'm not sure we even had thoughts of our own. We followed instructions without questioning. *Do not disappoint your elders; and whatever you do, don't ever talk back! And it doesn't matter if it is something you don't want to do, do it anyway. Never question the grown-ups, just do it*! Appearances meant everything. It was imperative to be a *nice* girl. I can't begin to count the times I heard, "*Your reputation and character are all you have; if you lose those, you don't have anything.*"

My daddy was the funniest man who ever lived, and his humor was exceeded only by his pride in his family. In today's market he would be the hottest commodity around as a standup comedian. His favorite line, without ever qualifying the statement, was to tell anyone who would listen that he had *female trouble*. Once, when he was quite ill and at an initial visit with a physician who had never seen him before, when asked what his problem was, Daddy replied, "Doc, I think I've got *female trouble*." After this doctor had treated Daddy for years and eventually learned that he lived in this family where he was the only male, the doctor agreed with him! Even the dogs and cats at our house seemed to also always be of the female variety!

Daddy traveled in his work and he was away from home almost all the time as were growing up. We would see him at Christmas and for an occasional weekend every few months or so when he would take time away from work to come home for a visit. He was not there for his wife nor his daughters, not for nurturing nor emotional support, to share neither the laughter nor the tears. He was there for nothing. He was away from all the responsibilities.

Sending home the bacon, the financial support, was the easy part. An envelope through the mail with the money order didn't take much effort on his part. It was the other part that he missed, and so did we. All of us needed his daily presence in our lives.

Mother was there, living her life through her children; never building a life for herself nor with her husband. She was in charge and we were one of the original single-parent families when divorce was infrequent, long before it became so common and widespread. In their marriage there was no divorce, only neglect; and we all suffered the consequences of this dysfunctional family.

The rare times Daddy was at home he would always say as he left us again, "You girls take care of your mother." I never failed to recognize the importance of that statement, that duty, which was another requirement of my perfection.

As I recall the times I saw my mother shed her silent tears when he left the driveway and I hid away and cried when he was leaving and I wanted him to stay, I was already aware that I had missed too much of my daddy in my life.

Only in his latter years as his health failed did Daddy return home to stay, and I wonder that he discovered too late how much he had lost. Even now, many years beyond his death, I am reminded often of what I lost through his daily absence from my growing-up years.

I remember once when I was in my twenties and waiting to go out on a date with my future husband, as I pranced in front of the mirror admiring myself in my new black dress, with my freshly applied makeup, bleached blonde hair, and long red nails, he looked at me longingly and said, "You don't look like my little Judy anymore." Okay, let me do it again. Of course, I didn't take what he said literally and understand it for what it was. No. I had to put my own interpretation on this and feel guilt for denying him the experience of having his *little Judy* still around now that he had returned home.

THE PERFECT SISTER

*B*eing fourth in a family of five daughters gave me the advantage of having older sisters to follow and from whom to learn and also to call on in life when needed. It also gave me the disadvantage of having to follow in their footsteps, for many times I found this was more of a burden than a blessing.

There we were, the stairsteps: Reba Ann, Barbara Jo, Beverly Watova, Judy Lee, and Linda Sue, known as *The Minnis Girls*, each with her own abilities and shortcomings; but always hidden back in that dark part of my mind I knew that shortcomings were not allowed. That was less than perfection, and not acceptable.

First there was Reba, the immaculate. All my life, up through and including today, my memories of her have been of cleaning house and cooking. Even when we were playing outside in our worlds of make-believe, she was keeping those pine straw walls straight and the dirt floors swept. As we

The Minnis Girls
Easter of 1944
(clockwise) Barbara, Reba, Beverly, Judy

were older, while the rest of us continued with our play, Reba moved indoors to keep house. I remember with laughter the many times I had to duck low and run fast to get out of the house and out of her way when I entered and she felt threatened that I would leave a fingerprint or speck of dirt behind in a spot of cleanliness just created by her.

As the oldest, Reba was the first to learn to drive; and, of course, the next three of us girls had to accompany her each time she ventured forth to learn and improve her driving skills.

As I look back on it now I can't decide whether mother was extremely lenient or exceptionally smart, for she did not go with us on these outings.

One day in particular, we all piled into the car and headed down the country road for Reba's driving lesson. Having been riding in automobiles all of our lives, we all knew how to drive and were freely giving Reba the benefit of our knowledge. As she approached a right-hand turn where she should have slowed down considerably before proceeding with the turn, if not stopped altogether, Barbara told her to push the gear into second and just go on. Dutifully, Reba did as instructed and almost killed us all as she made the turn on two wheels. When she finally recovered control of the automobile and herself, she proceeded home where she put us all out on the side of the road and thereafter did the remainder of her learning without us.

Second in this line of girls was Barbara, who was extremely talented and gifted. She was musically inclined; in fact, at one time she studied to become a concert pianist. From her pre-teen years she was the church pianist and/or organist and was known far and wide for her musical abilities. She taught many people to play the piano, and even had a blind student who also excelled under her tutelage.

Everything she attempted she did well. She was always the *teacher's pet* in school.

Barbara and Judy, ages 6 and 2
Fall of 1943

I vividly remember my first day in typing class in the tenth grade. As the teacher sat at her desk in front of the room she said to me, "You'll never be as good as your sister, Barbara." She was referring to the fact that Barbara, as her student, had won first place in typing from our local high school level through statewide competition.

Wasn't that a great start for my beginning of school that year? That was poor choice on the part of the teacher, not my sister. While I knew that, I still felt the pain of that moment and continually heard the replay of those words in my heart, almost like a whisper, "You'll never be as good as your sister."

However, in the competitive spirit myself, I did better than my sister that time, not only in typing but also in shorthand and all those other *office subjects*.

Why wasn't I surprised that this teacher never acknowledged my accomplishments?

And, help us all, Barbara even had naturally curly hair; and it was blonde, at that. Try following in those footsteps!

As we were growing up we had an honest-to-goodness, bona fide rain barrel at the corner of our home in the city which conveniently furnished unlimited water for our playhouse and was always a necessary commodity for our mudpies. Patient mother. We kept more spoons and pans from the kitchen in that playhouse than she had in the house.

These spoons and pans were only for mixing, though, and a Pepsi Cola bottle was for the dipping of water.

Being the youngest at that time I was, of course, quite the shortest. There was a large rock beside the rain barrel which I conveniently used as my stepping stone. On a warm summer day, when I was four years of age and Barbara was eight, I stepped on that stone, stood on my tiptoes and, since the water level was low, leaned well into the barrel, tilted the bottle sideways and waited for it to fill. I leaned a little too far and tumbled into the water, head first.

There I was, short little me, trapped in the rain barrel, obviously unable to call for help since my head was submerged in the water. My legs were flailing about as I unsuccessfully tried to get out. There was neither panic nor fear; and, without any fanfare, Barbara lifted me from the danger. Hand in hand we walked into the house, me looking like a drowned rat, and Barbara calmly beside me. When asked what had happened, Barbara simply said that I had fallen into the rain barrel, turned away, and went back outside to finish her mudpie.

I only wish I could have done the same for her years later.

I cherish the memory of the hours I spent at her side during that illness, both at her home and in the hospital. The peace we shared, just the two of us, Barbara and I, night after night in the absolute quiet of those hospital rooms is irreplaceable in my heart. I could talk and share with her, take care of her bodily needs, and walk hand in hand with her this time down memory lane, as only two sisters could do; but I couldn't lift her from illness and calmly walk away.

Next in line, smackdab in the middle of this set of five, was Beverly. The two of us were dubbed *The Golddust Twins,* and from infancy were almost inseparable.

We even cut each other's hair; well, not exactly. Those were the plans of two little girls, aged five and three. After Beverly had given me my haircut, leaving only four or five

The Golddust Twins
Beverly and Judy, ages 4 and 3

short, blonde hairs on my head (and mother reported that I came out of this looking like a coconut), she felt she was more experienced than I so instead of giving me my turn to now cut her hair, she did it herself. Straight in and out, everywhere she could reach, flat against the scalp, the scissors in those small hands snipped, snipped, snipped. When that haircut was finished, Beverly looked as if she were either designed as a checkerboard or patterned after a mangy dog.

Mother was so aggravated at Beverly that she gave her a spanking, while she could only laugh at me.

The only problem I had with Beverly was that she would abandon me to go and do things with the two older sisters in which I couldn't be

Beverly and Judy, ages 3 and 2, Summer of 1943

included. They would get together around the piano to perform at home and in public, playing and singing and making beautiful music. Anytime I tried to join, uninvited, of course, I would be ridiculed and laughed at by them for my less than perfect voice.

And don't you know that Beverly has a beautiful voice, that she took lessons from one of the best teachers in the southeast, performed in public for weddings and funerals and had all the solo parts in the church choir and in every performance from the school choir to the city symphony.

Her wedding day is vividly stamped into my memory. She married only six months before I, and this was a day of wonderful excitement for me. That is, until the actual event began; then, totally unexpected of myself, I began to cry. I shed so many tears during this happy event that it became quite a bit of entertainment to all in attendance, with the guests repeatedly asking how much I had been paid for my crying services. I would like to think those were tears of joy for

Beverly, but inside me somewhere I must have been feeling I was losing my best friend.

I can now realistically see that so much of this has been just what siblings naturally do to each other; but, through those years I only saw it as being less than perfect, and I knew I couldn't do that.

At the end of the line came Linda, our real live baby doll. She was born five days short of my sixth birthday, and when mother brought her home from the hospital she told me I could have the baby as my birthday present. We both know that I neither own nor possess her, but I accepted that gift quite seriously and still do; and that makes her just a little more precious in my life than my other sisters. I've jokingly told her through the years that the only spoiling I got was that she came along and spoiled my setup as the youngest child.

She was a tiny little thing, and we did treat her like another of our dolls. The good part was that this one could talk and play with me, but the bad part was she always cried when I pulled her hair.

Judy and Linda, ages 11 and 5

Judy and Linda, ages 9 and 3

When Linda passed her third birthday and still was unable to walk, mother took her to the doctor to find out what could possibly be wrong. He looked at us, told mother to make us put Linda down and to quit carrying her everywhere so she could learn to maneuver on her own. And with us being grounded from constant shuttle service for Linda, she conquered walking without assistance within two days.

Judy and Linda, ages 12 and 6, with Sissy, their cocker spaniel

Linda has never been a threat nor problem to me; she's my wonderful little sister, even all grown up.

CHAPTER 6

THE PERFECT NEIGHBOR

$\mathcal{T}$here's a definite beginning to being the perfect neighbor. First thing to do is listen and observe to find out what makes one appreciated and praised as *a wonderful neighbor.*

After a few years of marriage, our family of William, Judy, Kirby and Kevin moved into an antebellum neighborhood where we were already known, which is in the area of our church parish.

Within one week in that neighborhood I found out that the *nice lady down the street* baked cookies and came to the front doors in the neighborhood early afternoons with *a little something for you.* Immediately I posted this information into my mental file under the heading *THINGS I MUST DO TO BE THE PERFECT NEIGHBOR.*

We moved from that neighborhood seven years later without my ever once having baked and shared throughout the neighborhood those most delicious homemade cookies I had planned.

In looking back now it's interesting to remember that never during our seven years on that street did the *nice lady down the street* ever once bake and pass out homemade cookies, nor did anyone else. But I didn't see that then. I only knew that someday, somehow, someway, I was going to get those cookies baked and distributed throughout the neighborhood.

There was no time for baking these cookies during the summer because so much time was required for little league games and duties, Boy Scout activities, canning for the church bazaar, swimming lessons for the children, and family picnics. Then, of course, the PTA, class mother duties, and other activities commanded the school year.

When was I going to get time to do those cookies?

Couldn't do it at the holidays since we invite our friends and neighbors who would be alone on those days into our home for feasting and celebrating. Sometimes there are many friends present, sometimes less; but always our extra special friends, May Beard and Keith Huffstetter.

I recall one particular Thanksgiving when our southern weather was so warm the day of our dinner that we opened the doors and windows to allow us to light up the fireplace for the elderly ladies who looked forward to a cozy, warm fire on Thanksgiving.

And cookies certainly were out of the question during the most memorable Christmas we experienced during that time. All the invitations had been issued and preparations completed for our annual Christmas Dinner. Christmas day was as cold as the Thanksgiving had been warm. In fact, as we were preparing to attend Midnight Mass on Christmas Eve, one of our famous Canadian cold fronts passed through College Park and all the plumbing in our house froze and didn't thaw out for days.

Preparing dinner for family and guests with frozen water pipes was impossible, but we weren't going to be undone. The next day we just took our Christmas celebration to our neighborhood parish, St. John's Episcopal Church, and had an absolutely unforgettable dinner.

It so happened that Christmas fell on Sunday that year, so while the angels and archangels and all the company of heaven served upstairs, my husband and two sons set up tables in the church parlor. As the dinner cooked in the church kitchen we placed the fine linens, china, silver and crystal we had brought from home, and there's still talk at St. John's to this day about the year we celebrated the Christmas Eucharist to the rising aroma of baking turkey and dressing and steaming broccoli.

These Easter, Thanksgiving, and Christmas celebrations with our friends have become important annual events to us; and, to my dismay, all this wonder got lost in the shadow of those totally insignificant cookies that I never got around to making.

THE PERFECT VOLUNTEER

$\mathscr{T}$his is the spot where I could really strive for perfection. What a resume in this department! Beginning in early adulthood, I excelled in *volunteerism*.

The big event in our neighborhood in my twentieth year was the opening of the area hospital. Being relatively small and on a beginning budget, volunteers were critical to the early operation of this facility. Immediately my name went on the dotted line as one of the first volunteer *pink ladies* (that was uniform–wise, not skin color!). So began my career as a *professional* volunteer.

Being not content to just answer phones at the information desk or any of the other duties normally handled by these ladies, I moved beyond these assignments. Oh, I did these, too; but at the same time I went even further to encroach on what should have been performed by paid staff. I was trained to assist the pharmacist in filling prescriptions, even the protected narcotics. Due to the limited number of nursing staff and overabundance of patients, I assisted the physicians in the emergency room, including minor surgical procedures; and, I additionally substituted as ward clerk on any floor that needed me. Television installation became an area of expertise, and you should have seen me scooping ice and pouring juice for patients just before their bedtime!

I received a pin for five hundred hours of volunteer service earned during only six months time, and was given special recognition as outstanding volunteer.

Are we now getting close to that stage of perfection?

This was followed by years of volunteer experience, which was in addition to all the other responsibilities I was handling day by day.

Not only did I attend and participate in scheduled meetings and activities of my volunteer groups, I also held office in each of these as president or secretary or committee chairperson or such, and thereby assumed additional responsibilities within each organization. I served in elected positions of governing boards, appointed positions and those for which I simply volunteered my services as member. I spearheaded the reorganization of a defunct high school parent teacher organization, then became its president. Both the list and the responsibilities of the activities in which I participated is overwhelming.

For years I had kept myself busy being super person, being in control, and always striving to do more than my allocated time could ever permit. If I kept myself totally involved doing for others, then I wouldn't have to recognize what was happening to me. If I didn't have time to look at my life, I wouldn't have to admit that it was out of control. Finally, I discovered that the most impossible thing I ever had to live up to was my own expectations of myself.

THE PERFECT HOUSEKEEPER
(WHICH I'LL NEVER BE)

My least favorite subject. First, let me emphasize that I hate housework! This comes to you from a renegade female. My mother and sisters are the complete opposite. And, my Lord, how bored I get in listening to anyone tell of how they dusted and vacuumed and washed loads of laundry and swept and mopped and changed the filters and changed the linens and cooked and washed dishes and on and on and on and on. The very thought makes me nauseous. With all the floors throughout our home being carpeted, I don't even own a mop, and only have a broom for the necessity of brushing away dirt from the sidewalk leading to the front door. When it obviously needs to be done, my husband and I will together manage to completely vacuum the house, including all the furniture.

I still cannot figure out nor discover from the scriptures why God ever created so much dust. Are you aware of how much faster you can remove dust from all furniture with the vacuum and those neat attachments, as opposed to cloth, spray-on fruit-scented polish and elbow-grease? I see no point in chasing dust on a daily basis.

We keep things clean enough for the health department to stay away from the front door and they probably couldn't get to the back door because of all the dogs we have out there. All they would have to put up with out front is two cats, now reduced from our former population of seven felines.

Rather than giving the furniture an extra coat of polish, we prefer to spend our time sitting in the swing in the backyard while looking across the lake as the dogs knock their fleas at our feet.

At the risk of offending my *save the ecology* friends, I wish everything involved in housekeeping were disposable. I remember reading several years ago about a famous movie star who had satin sheets and pillowcases on her bed and each was removed for disposal daily after only one use. I don't ever want to find out this wonderful story is not true. I can think of only one thing more delightful and that would be to have the entire bedroom replenished daily; by hired help, of course!

The sister Reba is almost six feet tall, and one of the few people who ever sees the top of my refrigerator. It used to be every time she came to my house she would invariably comment on how that needed to be cleaned. I finally suggested to her that she could feel free to bring supplies with her and clean this if it bothered her that much, for it certainly wasn't that important to me.

The last time she was at our house her one outstanding statement about the visit was, "Well, I see Judy still isn't a housekeeper." That was the day of interment of our sister, Barbara, and we had all met at our house for family time together after the funeral.

Our sons and friends have always seemed to be happy in our less than perfect house, and that's enough for us. When

I'm dead and gone someone else can remove any remaining dust bunnies from beneath the beds and furniture.

I do like to iron, though. Don't ask me to vacuum or dust, but I'll gladly spend hours at the ironing board. Maybe that's my one redeeming virtue in this world of cleanliness.

Kevin has observed that in my life *summer creases* are not to be tolerated. You know, *summer creases*: those things commonly referred to as wrinkles, *sum mer* here, *sum mer* there.

THE PERFECT PARENT

One of the delightful parts of being a parent is to be given the opportunity for a repeat trip through childhood. And it's even better the second time around because we know the surprises our little ones are approaching as we hold their hands for that little while.

The best advice I have received in my entire life was from the boys' pediatrician when they were still quite young and I was trying to raise perfect children. Dr. John Allen told me, "Do what's best for today, and tomorrow will take care of itself." In my role as a mother, I liberally used this. How could I have had that wonderful knowledge and not used it for myself when it was working so well for our sons.

I was lucky to not have to be a working mother outside our home for several years from the birth of our sons until they were well into school; then, I worked only part-time jobs for the most part, which allowed us to have many good experiences together. I think the expression now is *quality time*.

Kirby, with learning disabilities and hearing impairment, needed special attention and he was able to get the best training available anywhere in the educational system at the Atlanta Speech School, a private institution with a self-contained program for learning disabled and hearing impaired children. Through a program offered under the auspices of the school I was able to be a classroom aide there which provided partial tuition for Kirby, again enabling me to forego securing full-time employment.

We, like most of the families involved in the school, resided quite a distance away. Kevin was enrolled during those years at The Village School, a small private facility nearby, putting mother and sons in the same area while daddy went to work daily at his job.

We traveled back and forth in our little red Volkswagen and have fond memories of *Paul Harvey and the Rest of the Story* on the car radio as we daily worked our way home through the afternoon rush hour traffic.

We also learned about the birds, if not the bees, as we rode the miles early every morning to watch the pattern of the days when the birds took flight in the mornings and of the seasons as they went further south and again returned.

William returned home from work early in the afternoons and had dinner prepared and on the table for us when we arrived a couple of hours later.

The entire lot of us, being full of humor, feel personal ownership of April Fools Day. One particular April First the boys and I returned home at the end of our long day to find our meal on the table, with each plate containing Gainesburger dog food and potato peelings, accompanied by glasses of dishwater. Hamburgers, french fries, and cokes at the fast-food restaurant provided a somewhat improved meal that evening.

Then there was the year that Kevin got a special treat for his lunch at school on April Fools Day. The students were required to *brown bag* lunch from home. I had packed his lunch that morning with only one sandwich, which was 'specially prepared by placing one sheet of paper containing the words "April Fool" between two pieces of bread. That was all, nothing else. When he opened his bag at lunchtime the joke was thoroughly enjoyed by Kevin, his teacher and the entire school population. In fact, all the teachers and other students chipped in part of their lunches for Kevin and he had a veritable feast.

Every age and stage of these two sons enhanced my classification as mother, and no one could be more pleased with nor proud of anyone as I am with the two young men I warmly call my sons.

But even this most wonderful part of my life had to carry guilt.

A few short weeks after the birth of my second child, when the first was only a few days beyond his first birthday, my mother was visiting with us one day and told me that even with five children close together in years she never had two children in diapers at the same time. Yes, I had two children in diapers at that time; and, with my mother giving me this information I had to assume I was doing something wrong, and this was cause for a major guilt trip for me.

One more time I wasn't listening to what was being said. Instead of taking this as a criticism of what I was or wasn't doing, I should have heard and acknowledged what my mother had done. I can now see that she considered this an extraordinary accomplishment on her part; but, in my limited span of vision at that time, I took it rather as a criticism and erroneously overloaded myself with guilt.

After we finally got beyond that diaper stage, though, there has been so much love and caring and fun and laughter and wonder in this role that I never had time to think about what I might be doing wrong. Being a mother has been a major event of my life and a joy beyond comparison.

My sons. I held their hands for a little while, they hold my heart forever.

THE PERFECT WIFE

*H*ow do I tell of being a wife without speaking of my husband? No one anywhere doesn't like William. He is the kindest, most gentle, loving, secure, and realistic man in the world. I, as his wife, and his two sons come before anyone or anything else in his life. He is completely devoted to his family. I'm the luckiest woman in the world to be his wife. Notice I didn't say he is perfect, because he isn't; but he sure is a good husband. If he were perfect, he wouldn't get so aggravated with my dogs and cats!

We were married in June of 1969, and from that moment forward I have been proud to be his wife and then to later be the mother of his sons.

William and I have taken the foundation of our love and built upon that our marriage, which will stand against even the strongest forces as blown by the winds of life.

Because of the patience of my husband, not necessarily myself, we don't argue or fuss with each other. We usually

William and Judy in May of 1982. The PTA President at age 40, Judy thought she had to be the gray-haired, overweight wife and mother

are in agreement on most of the important things, and have found that the insignificant doesn't matter anyway. William's philosophy in life is *KEEP IT SIMPLE*; and, with this, he has been a tremendous, positive influence for me. We enjoy each other's company and spend as much time together as possible, and not a day goes by that we don't each remind the other of our love.

This love and support from my husband which I never doubted was there for me eventually enabled me to reach

William and Judy with son, Kirby, ten years later in May of 1992, at a church sponsored, Hawaiian-theme dinner. Judy, at age 50, still the overweight wife and mother, but back to blonde hair, and now President of the Church Women's Group.

within myself and work through the feelings I encountered when I felt I had betrayed my promises to him as I was attracted to another man outside my marriage.

See there. I always knew I would never be perfect, and this was the most positive proof.

At the time of this attraction which I was experiencing, my husband and I had within recent years experienced the divorce of two marriages of friends with whom we were

Ten months later, on March 25, 1993, celebrating William's birthday at Paradise Cove Luau, Honolulu, Hawaii. Judy, at age 51, with a new attitude, 100 pounds lighter, now President of her own company, and happier than she ever dreamed possible!!!

closely associated, each of these being of more than twenty years duration. Both instances were quiet shocking and disturbing to us individually and as a couple. Suddenly we had realized even happy marriages weren't necessarily immune to outside influences and divorce. That was very much in my thoughts when I finally acknowledged this attraction.

    I was now forced to look at my own marriage, almost microscopically, for the first time since it had begun more than twenty years earlier. Through this inspection I sadly lost my storybook romance, but wonderfully found its strength and stability which enabled us to work through this together.

William is a quiet and gentle man, the same as he has been from the point of our meeting; whereas, I, on the other hand, was quite the extrovert when we met. Through our years together I subdued my personality to try to match the quietness of my husband, not because he wanted me to do so, but because I was constantly attempting to be what I thought others wanted me to be. I was never secure enough to just be myself, always looking to be *Little Miss Perfect* for everyone else.

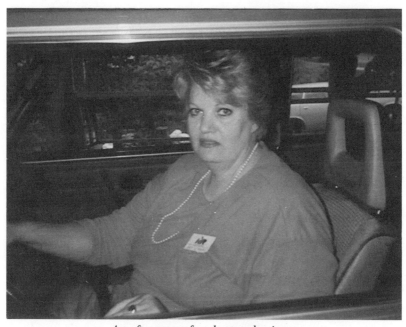

An afternoon of real estate business

I love to dance, William doesn't. At a beautiful Christmas party during the time of my part-time real estate career, the broker of the firm with which I was affiliated danced with every woman at that party except me. There I sat, silently crying inwardly but giving off the message, "Don't ask me to dance, I'm ecstatically happy sitting here quietly with my husband."

In retrospect, I now know that while William might not have been just as happy to sit there and watch me dance without him, the world certainly would not have come to an early end if I had gone ahead and enjoyed myself by dancing with another man.

THE PERFECT CHRISTIAN

I could picture it! I knew exactly how it was going to be! The throne of gold. Huge. Sparkling in the bright sunlight. There upon the square pillow of ecclesiastical purple sat God Almighty, wearing his soft, cream colored silk robe, His long, grey beard and grey hair sparkling clean, reflecting the prisms of light. Upon His lap rested the open book in which was recorded, in God's own handwriting, every sin of every person who had ever been. He clasped the book in both hands, looked towards the line of people in front of Him, and began to call names and read aloud.

Everything in my life pointed to Judgement Day. That was the grand destination, and this was it. Today was the day of days, and I was going to now answer personally for everything I had ever done wrong. Every sin. Every thought or act of imperfection. The line of people stretched beyond imagination, yet every person there could see and hear every sound from the lips of God as He began to call the roll and enumerate the sins. Of course, I was the first in line and my sins would be read aloud by God to be heard by every person there, so that no one would miss my imperfection. And my parents stood on either side of me so they would know without doubt everything I had ever done wrong. No need to try to conceal anything of imperfection in my life and think they would not know, for it would all be read by God Himself before them on Judgement Day, and I couldn't disappoint anyone. That was not allowed. So I absolutely had to be perfect!

And this little girl was so terribly frightened by this eventual day of judgement that fear crushed her life for years and years even beyond childhood, and the pain of imperfection became so unbearable that she finally had to face it if she would survive.

PART THREE

TODAY

MUSIC SOOTHES A BROKEN SPIRIT

*B*eing exposed to the symphony, classical music, and even being in attendance at the birth of Rock and Roll was enjoyable in my life, but my favorite has always been country music. We didn't have television in our home until I was a teenager but we were always tuned in to the radio.

Unlike the televised coverage of the actual events of the war in the Persian Gulf, radio gave small details of World War II. Even though I was less than four years of age at the time, I profoundly recall the radio announcement of the end of that war. With shouts of jubilation and tears of joy, people from every walk of life rushed outdoors to embrace each other and share their uncontained happiness and relief. There was a spontaneous parade up and down the sidewalks in our neighborhood to celebrate that event and I distinctly remember riding my tricycle round and round the rejoicing adults who were dancing in the driveways and walkways.

Judy, age 4

I fondly remember when we had fifteen-minute radio
programs late afternoons with James and Martha Carson, that
mother daily listened to her soap-box opera "Pepper Young's
Family" as she cooked the evening meal; and, as we took turns
washing and drying the dishes after supper we would spend
the evenings with The Lone Ranger, Fibber Megee and Molly,
and The Shadow.

Who can ever forget "*The Louisiana Hayride*" or the
crackly music which was picked up on Saturday nights as the
"*Grand Old Opry*" came across the miles, when we heard
Hank Williams, Farron Young, Ernest Tubbs, Ferlon Huskey,
Patsy Cline, Red Foley, Kitty Wells, George Morgan, Hank

Snow, and the greatest county music singer of all time, Jim Reeves.

No wonder I still prefer radio over television or the movie theatres.

Country music continues to be very important in my life, and nothing is sweeter to my ears now than the music of Reba McEntire or Garth Brooks, the crystal clear voice of that beautiful, versatile lady named Lorrie Morgan, and always and forever, Gentleman Jim Reeves.

How wonderful, also, to experience the joy of the contagious fun and laughter of the precious Dolly Parton.

And how about one very sexy Collin Raye in those tight jeans! UMP!! Sparkly eyes. Winning smile. Warm personality. Incredible talent. Voice of rare beauty. No doubt about it, that's one fine man. With his absolutely fantastic singing, he has fast become one of my favorites. I have yet to find even one song he sings that I don't like. Through his music he brings me much joy, and through his success he exemplifies what I, too, can accomplish by hard work, perseverance and determination. And his band is likewise noteworthy, too, with the ability that's there. It does me good to see these fellows enjoy their work so much.

As far as I am concerned, *The Dance*, by Tony Arata, is the greatest and strongest song ever written and performed. The infinitely profound story in these lyrics is of a simple dance. A once-in-a-lifetime, breathless moment of joy just might have been self-denied if the dancer had foreseen the sad conclusion of the relationship about which he sings. The undeniable beauty of this song shows that it is better to dance and fall than never to dance at all.

This recording by Garth Brooks was released and available to me as a comfort when I was seeking so many answers, when I was just attempting to hold my own ground and continuing as I progressed forward, however slow and painful the journey. Within hours of my sister's death, this song became my solace. Almost constantly I wound and rewound this tape for months, as I listened to the words over and over again, day and night; and *The Dance* is now gently woven as a beautiful ribbon through my life.

It seemed my emotional stability was dependent upon those words for a very long time. I knew my pain, and I likened that dance to being representative of life. While the pain I was experiencing was almost unbearable, I knew that I would not have given up having had experienced the love of these others just to forego the pain.

During this time of seemingly unsurmountable turmoil I found untold consolation in country music. Who would ever have thought I would have unsuspectingly found so many answers this way.

With questions to be faced and decisions to be made, invariably answers unexpectedly came to me numerous times through the words of a song as I popped a tape into the car radio, put in place the earphones of my little radio at work, or heard the music at home.

Here I was, engulfed in this infatuation, still trying to avoid the words of my priest, "You have to consider divorce is a possibility" when, one night as I was driving home from work in the quiet of the after–midnight hour, my automobile was filled with the voice of Reba McEntire as she pushed against my conscience with her words, *"You're the first time I've thought about leaving him, I really don't know what I'll do."*

Did I ever sit bolt upright and take notice! This just kept coming back over and over again. No matter what I did, it wouldn't stay away.

This pain inside me had to be faced. I could no longer put off nor ignore this situation, hoping it would take care of itself and go away. That obviously was not going to happen. Gradually I began to unwrap the package and look closely at the contents, acknowledging the attraction to myself for what it represented.

Slowly I came to the realization that I did not need to feel guilty for having natural human emotions. That thought emphatically hit me out of the quietness, and I understood. This was not the first time in my life I had encountered these feelings.

Several years before I met my husband I had met another young man with whom I had shared an attraction the same as I had with my husband and which I now felt for this other man. I had not felt guilty when I had these feelings before I was married, so why now? Can emotions be turned on and off like a water faucet? Do they end just because a wedding ceremony occurs? Aren't these feelings there within us for a purpose? They happen with neither encouragement nor anticipation. So, it's okay. Take it for what it is and accept that you're human.

In that moment, with the simple acceptance of that knowledge, accompanied by neither magic nor spectacular fireworks, the accumulation of years of bottled up guilt began to slowly, quietly and gently fall away; then, with the speed and haste of a well placed intricate design of dominoes, the release gathered speed as it rapidly and swiftly and surely tumbled out of my life.

But even with that release, as wonderful as it was, I wasn't yet at the end of my search. This journey was still underway.

Months later, I was listening to a tape of music, again by Reba, and heard the words that time, "*You can take the wings off me.*" That was it, my moment of truth. I rewound that tape, and as I again listened to the words I realized that I had unconsciously reached up to my shoulders with both hands and was literally *pushing* away my wings, my wings of perfection. And with that movement, I was released. Oh, how sweet that freedom. I had already dropped my baggage of guilt and as my spirits lifted upward, it was incredible that I soared higher than could have been dreamed possible. My wings fell away and I never looked back to see where they had landed, for that didn't matter.

What did matter was that through that experience I found more than I would ever have dared to ask, or dream, or think, or hope or imagine. I flew with Jonathan Livingston Seagull. If you've never met him, you'll find him resting on a shelf in the local library in a book written by Richard Bach; that is, if he's not above the cliffs with me.

Several years ago Jonathan set the example for me when he found within himself that which urged him to push beyond the limits and lose those ideas which had kept him earthbound.

Yet, even with this significant turn in the road, there were still obstacles and detour signs in the way of the completion of this journey. My destination was getting closer, but I still had miles yet to travel before this search would end.

A Course In First Aid

All my grown-up life I had secretly known that there was a double standard for me. I could not do the things I wanted to do, to simply have an enjoyable day and at the same time please others. I always felt that if I pleased myself that my behavior, actions, attitude, my everything, would not be what was expected of me.

How could I be a free-spirited, fun-loving, carefree person and also be responsible at the same time?

The only exception to this was in my role as a mother! How wonderful the innocent love and acceptance of my children. For others, I felt I had to subdue my personality, my desires, my life, in order that they would not be disappointed in me. That door has now opened to show me I can do both; and further to know that if someone is disappointed in me that's their problem, not mine. I like Kirby's summation, "It sounds like a personal problem to me." I have only to live my life for me, not for anyone else.

In my life, I take responsibility. No one ever forced me. I took my own personal experiences, misread and incorrectly interpreted the signals, then programmed myself with guilt and reaped the rewards of all these errors. As I fed the guilt hidden deeply inside my being I gained the weight. I didn't know that I was feeding guilt until I found the answers in my search. Losing weight was an unexpected bonus.

In this search I found the secret of living with myself, with others, and with God. I had to first accept my limitations and then have realistic expectations of myself as well as others.

Life does not require me to be self-sufficient, yet at the same time I must be self-reliant.

God never expected me to be perfect. He allows space for making mistakes so I do not need to require perfection of myself. He has forgiveness for me so I must be able to forgive myself the same as I forgive others.

Once the formula for this was learned I found true happiness as I had never known before. I can be both carefree and responsible. I need only to keep these in balance.

The emotions of repressed feelings, like the fermentation of processing wine, must be allowed to breathe. Neither can be kept stopped up forever or the cork will blow.

I could want to not overeat but that was never enough. First, I had to find the key to unlock my mind and heart and release the guilt before the cure would work.

I couldn't just apply a bandaid to this terrible pain in my life; I had to completely cleanse the wound before the healing process would begin.

Once I took the step to accomplish this, my weight plummeted with the swiftness and sureness of a skydiver, flying free and yet upheld by the surety of happiness which became my parachute to hold me safely and to gently take me to the end of the jump. I've landed on my feet and am enjoying today and all it has to offer me without guilt. What a journey this has been. What a landing. And, oh, what happiness and fullness.

I'm not God, I am only me, and my creations are no more complex than *papier mache*. Unlike the children's game, I don't even have to wear a blindfold as I face my own monsters. All I have to do is take my stick and whack them face-to-face. Sound simple? It is! It's only when I try to make life complicated that resistance and trouble are encountered. Remember to keep it simple. What better way is there?

In my preteen years, attending church weekly without fail, we would open Sunday School assembly with the song, *"Others, Lord, yes, others, let this my motto be. Lord, let me live for others that I might live like Thee."*

Judy, age 7, going to Sunday School

Sunday morning
Winter of 1946
(clockwise) Reba, Mother, Barbara, Beverly and Judy

These words were imprinted in my mind and I had lived them day by day from those Sundays forward, but no longer. No longer. No longer would I live my life through others.

Daughter, sister, student, employee, date, bride, friend, wife, mother, volunteer, Christian, neighbor, housekeeper: these roles are all part of me, but are not me. Without hurting others, I can live life for myself. First I am, and should be, me.

WHAT IS BEST FOR MYSELF

One day in conversation with a friend, as we were discussing a situation concerning his employment, he said to me, "I have to do what is best for myself."

While that instance may not have been the first time those words were ever spoken in my presence, this was, without doubt, the very first time I had ever actually heard this phrase and recognized that this possibility also existed for me. Most important, this became the point when I understood it is permissible for me to do things which I consider are best for myself, to know I can likewise do this in my own life.

There are three groups of people in this world: those who make things happen, those who let things happen, and those who stand there and ask what happened.

Without trying to be in control, I can take charge and be responsible for myself. And that I must do.

If I would make life happen for me, I had to give up my garbage. Completely give it up. Throw it all away. In com-

puter language it's garbage in/garbage out; in life it's the re-
verse, garbage out/non-garbage in. I couldn't keep even one
scrap. That meant no more self-pity, repressed anger, hate
nor guilt. No more being the martyr. I simply only had to
accept life in the complete joy and happiness and love of
myself and others.

Once I opened my eyes to look beyond the superfluous, I
found what is real. Happiness replaced pain, and all I had to
do was accept it.

Because of what I've experienced I'm somewhat taken
by surprise when I see workshops advertised whereby one
can *take control*, and this usually seems to be directed towards handling stress.

My salvation came in *turning loose*, when I finally realized and accepted there was nothing I could control. If I
cannot control the rising of the sun or moon, the movement
of the winds, the ebb and flow of the tides, the growing of
the trees, or the changing of the seasons, how could I ever
control anything as complex as my human body and soul?

The moment I came to that realization I no longer attempted to resurrect and repair my shelf for I no longer needed
it nor anything that had been stored there. Then I knew that
not only should there never have been that shelf in my life
but also that I should have faced, handled as I could, and
then tossed out any leftovers. I didn't need to keep residual
from any of these even in anticipation of tomorrow.

Removing that shelf and all it held allowed me to find
within myself what has always been there, that which had
been concealed by all the clutter I had accumulated.

I finally found the strength and courage for today, knowledge that today is all I'm promised or need, and to enjoy today as I want to without guilt. I've learned to ask the questions and then accept the answers that come and not to try
to force the answers I want. I cannot control life, I can only
experience it.

Once I opened myself I was truly astounded to find that the answers had been there all the time. I was so much in control and trying to force the answers which I wanted that I couldn't find the correct information.

The finding of my answers was an unparalleled and beautiful experience. When I turned loose and took off the blinders I had put on my life, the answers continuously appeared. I found them at different times in different places and through different people and in different events. If I had not made these discoveries as I did, they would have surfaced elsewhere.

I had to open my mind and become receptive to the truth before I could see clearly. Through this simple act, I finally realized that what I was seeking had been there all the time. I just never could distinguish this before because I was always trying to force my own solutions.

Even as far as I have progressed, my recovery is yet underway and I continuously make discoveries about life and myself. How many *ah-ha's* are allowed before I'm blinded by the wonders of life!

With the absence of my monsters I'm now as an empty vessel with space to receive the correct information. What a blessing!

As I made that second trip through childhood with those two wonderful boys called my sons, it was good to renew acquaintances with Winnie the Pooh and Mickey and Minnie, experience Star Wars, be introduced to Fievel, read again about the little train that could, visit with that nice neighbor Mr. Rogers, and travel those afternoons on Sesame Street.

Of all the old and new friends I ran into this time, the best was meeting the incredible E.T. Now, I don't know how E.T. appears among siblings and contemporaries back on his planet, but here on earth he sure didn't blend in with anyone else. Yet, even E.T. is perfect, just as you and I are also perfect.

What an absolutely thrilling experience it was when I discovered myself and finally figured out that with all my flaws and warts, and, yes, even with those extra pounds I carried, I am perfect–because I am the only one of me there is or ever will be.

That's not to say I am perfect in my relationships with others, nor that my health is perfect, nor that anything else about my life outside myself is perfect. I found out I am *me*, and that is enough. As the pattern I am perfect, it is only as the finished product that I am not yet complete and am in a state of imperfection.

There's a picture that's photocopied, thumbtacked and taped around many desks in offices in this area which shows a sad looking child with the caption *BE PATIENT – GOD IS NOT FINISHED WITH ME YET*.

I do not like that. If I am a child of God and created in His image, am I not created in perfection? It's not God that isn't finished with me, it's me who is not finished with myself. I am the one who put the imperfections into my life, not God.

A PIECE OF CAKE

I have often remarked that more calories travel through the break room on a daily basis in the department where I work than goes through any public restaurant in that area.

I knew without a doubt that I had arrived in my commitment to change my attitude towards food and lose weight the day of a baby shower for one of the employees there who was soon going on maternity leave. This day was early in the time of my weight loss, and rather than expose myself to the temptation of unwanted calories I chose to just skip the festivities.

You know, of course, that a well meaning coworker returned to our work area with a piece of cake for me. That piece of cake was the choice corner section, the part with the extra icing and even one of the pretty, edible roses made of icing. I graciously thanked her for the kindness in remembering me and as soon as she turned her back I took that cake-filled napkin in hand, walked across the hallway to the restroom and tossed napkin and cake, icing and all, into the toilet and flushed it away without even one small morsel having gone into my mouth.

I finally knew that I could have my cake and wear it too, and I wasn't going to do that any longer.

PHYSICAL COMPLICATIONS

s I was approaching this time in my journey, I began undergoing medical testing for some health problems I was experiencing. On an almost daily basis, accompanied by my husband, I was in consultation or examination by one of several doctors which were treating me, at a laboratory for x-rays or blood tests or some other strange experience in the name of medical research. Finally, after weeks of these seemingly constant microscopic evaluations, terminal illness was at least ruled out, even though a painful, rheumatic, chronic syndrome of the connective tissue was diagnosed. Surgery was also scheduled for yet another condition which needed to be corrected.

What should have been a simple procedure with two to three weeks recovery continued into months. I awoke from this surgery in acute pain and incapacitated with symptoms totally unrelated to the surgical procedure I had just undergone. Incorrect initial diagnosis only added to the length of the recuperation.

During a period of several months following this surgery I had more than sixty prescriptions with equally as many medical office visits for treatments.

Two months beyond the date of the original surgery I underwent a second procedure to correct a spinal injury which was the eventual correct diagnosis.

Pain, medication, and medical treatments, enhanced by physical therapy, continued.

At an appointment almost three months following the second surgery, I received sixteen injections into my back and spine in an effort to relieve the pain which continued. Less than twenty-four hours later the surgeon told me a third surgery was possible because of complications from the second surgery.

I didn't want any more surgery. I didn't want to see another doctor or hospital or physical therapist or lab assistant or nurse or anesthesiologist or even a medical receptionist. I didn't want to have another x-ray or MRI or laboratory test of any kind. I didn't want to swallow another pill or be stuck with another needle or experience one more moment of pain or frustration with this recovery. So I just gave up. At that moment I was ready to willfully die, and I just leaned against the wall and cried.

And what I found from that moment was totally unexpected.

I knew when my sister died that I was angry at her for daring to give up in her fight for survival; therefore, I blamed her and not the cancer for the death. I knew that anger was yet inside me but I had no idea of how deep it had penetrated into my soul. My struggle was totally insignificant compared to what hers had been. The difference was that she had to acknowledge there was no hope for her.

As I touched bottom in my pit of despair that day I once again met that anger; then, like an illumination in the dark from the flame of a small candle, I understood her struggle and acceptance of death, and this anger gently dissipated. I also then, in that instant, saw and knew my emotional dependence upon this other man for what it had been.

With this knowledge and a movement as soft and quiet as the fluttering of the wings of a butterfly taking flight on a warm summer day, I released the insatiable emotional ties with which I had bound myself to him. This time I silently cried tears of relief and peace.

Then, as unbelievable as anything I had found in this search, I suddenly found that I was also very angry with this man. Now where had that been hiding? Even greater than the *where*, though, was the *why*.

In the nightmares I could take care of neither my sister nor this man and again they abandoned me, both through death this time. Could that have come from not being able to take care of them in life, not being able to control their situations, not being able to make everything perfect for these two very important people in my life?

THE LIGHTHOUSE

*D*on't think I lost weight because of illness. Try staying at home, confined indoors for the better part of four months, going outside only for medical appointments, daily walks, and three short trips to drop off insurance forms at the office, always accompanied by someone else since I was unable to drive an automobile for more than six months following the initial surgery.

During my illness, sharing this story became paramount to my continued weight loss and the recovery of my health; but my motivation is foremost and always there, penetrating every fiber of my being.

This motivation softly stirred in the air created by the turning of the ceiling fans as I lay in bed day after day during the months of my recuperation, it was plastered against the yawning cavity of the open refrigerator door, and it constantly sat inside those cupboards and microwave oven.

In my life, too, the temptation to yield to over–indulgence of food is at times also monstrous, but I'm overjoyed to know that these times are now few and far between. No longer do I think of food every waking moment.

The major change in my diet was simply that I finally put food in its proper perspective and adapted healthy eating habits into my lifestyle.

With all the hours spent working we do not have time for grocery shopping, cooking and dishwashing at home. Through necessity we've found some local restaurants in our area which specialize in serving vegetables at a very reasonable price, and in our daily schedule William and I can take thirty minutes to sit down and enjoy each other's company while we're served a delicious meal. For less than ten dollars we can both have a full meal with leftovers to take to work with us for our evening meal. With our schedules, we sleep through the breakfast hours and have found it convenient to supplement our daily diet with fresh fruits and plenty of water. There's nothing magical nor special nor mind boggling about the change in what I now eat. It's that I now keep it simple!

Someone once told me that half of life is *IF*. I prefer to look at what is left when the *IF* is removed from life, and that is reality. That's what I had to deal with and quit functioning on emotions. I found my weakness was guilt, guilt from not being perfect. This could have just as well been fear, anger, hurt, self-pity, denial, or any other self–defeating attitude. The important thing was to find my hidden, self–destructive emotion and let go of it.

I turned loose of the guilt which was holding me down and when I released those wings of perfection I soared. Better than that, I soared to heights beyond any possible dream.

In the few short weeks between the turning loose of the guilt and this release of my expectations of self–perfection, when I had without any conscious effort on my part dropped more than twenty pounds of the excess weight which I was carrying on my body I began to look closely and realistically at how I was functioning in life. For the very first time I stripped away all the pretensions and came face to face with myself.

Through this self examination I decided that I no longer wanted to be fat. I acknowledged there is something I want to do in my life which is hindered by this weight, and I want the remainder of my life to be the best years of my life.

In my soul searching I found a very personal and private reason for continuing to lose weight. This motivation is planted firmly in front of me and I reach to it often. As a ship will look to the lighthouse, I turn often to face this beacon. I will never lose sight of this purpose.

That commitment remained intact and was always present with me even during those days of convalescence. The opportunity to overeat was very much available to me those days and nights, as it is also there for me since I've returned to the world outside, but I continue to hold to my motivation for the weight loss and to keep off the weight once it has been taken off. Most important, my motivation removed and replaced the self–pity and martyrdom of presumed sacrifice. My lifeboat continues to hold me afloat and won't capsize as long as I remember to hold onto this motivation.

I know that only because of the strength I had already found was I able to survive the extended illness I experienced. No one could have asked for more support than my husband and sons gave to me during those months of confinement, but there was no way possible that they could be there every moment. Shorty, Kirby's Yorkshire Terrier, napped under my bed and took every step with me when I ventured forth from my bed; while Cuddles, our independent, fourteen-year-old, loveable cat alternately took naps on the bed with me or on the window ledge. Waggles, Kevin's Cocker Spaniel, and Jody, our Sheltie, stood constant guard outside the glass doors as I was upstairs in the bedroom or downstairs in the sitting room. These three faithful dogs were my constant, loyal companions but they, too, were limited in their contributions. Many times in the dark hours of the night, as I would lie in my bed unable to sleep, I would enjoy a smile and chuckle as the ducks at the dock beyond my bedroom window would begin their chatter which resounded across the yard like spontaneous laughter. The telephone became my lifeline to the outside world, and I became finely tuned to the sounds of the postman's vehicle. It needed a brake job, but I would have missed that squeak if repairs had been made.

There were times I would become depressed or lonely or simply overwhelmed with it all, when it seemed I would just never be well enough to do even the simple things of life again. Almost as if someone sensed my needs at these times, without fail there would always be contact either from my Delta or Parish family. The telephone would ring with the cheery voice of one of my coworkers or fellow parishioners, there would be cards in the mailbox, or the doorbell would ring for the delivery of flowers.

These contacts opened up my life again and now I once more embrace friends with a blessed closeness. Even though I was being social through the years, I had pushed others away from my life and in this way created selective isolation.

The nurture and caring of my husband, my sons, my mother, my friends, and my Delta and St. John's Parish families was a very rich experience which took me away from the cdgc and became part of my return to the fullness of life. And I thank God for each and every one of these wonderful people who continually enrich my daily walk through life.

I could never have made this journey alone, and Collin Raye beautifully sings the message I would give to each and every companion who traveled with me.

> *Let the world stop turning, Let the sun stop burning,*
> *Let them tell me love's not worth going through,*
> *If it all falls apart, I'll know deep in my heart,*
> *In this life I was loved by you.*

I will be forever grateful for what each did for me.

BLOOM WHERE YOU ARE PLANTED

I smile warmly with love at the remembrance of my wonderful husband and his understanding throughout my journey.

Without fail, William constantly supported and urged me to bloom into the person I could be. He encouraged, he nudged, and he gently pushed me to do things alone, to step out and experience life for myself. He told me I didn't need him to always be there to hold my hand, that I could make and live with my own decisions. The most important thing he said to me was that I did not have to always tell him or anyone else of everything I knew or thought or did. That sounds so extremely small and insignificant, but this one statement became the single most important release for me to be an individual.

The beautiful, sultry voice of Wynonna Judd lovingly gives us a song co-written by her mother which opens with the words, "*Keeper of the gates of wisdom, please let me in.*" That person has to be my husband.

Through the years I have often marveled and commented to my friends and family of his wisdom, but he always reminds me it is just the application of his philosophy to "Keep it simple."

When I was involved in illness and so completely frustrated with the continuing pain and seemingly evasive recovery, John Anderson sent me another very important answer in his current release being played on radio. I really liked the song and should have known when I kept listening for it over and over again that there was going to be a message for me somewhere in those words. My husband in his infinite love and understanding would hold me in a tender embrace many times as I would, in tears, listen to the song.

Let go of the stone, if you don't want to drown
In the sea of heartache that's dragging you down,
It's pulling you under and you keep hanging on,
If I'm ever gonna save you, let go of the stone.
Put your arms around me and swim with me to
*   shore.*
Just let go of that old memory, I know it's hard to do,
But I'll be here holding on to you.
If I'm ever gonna save you, let go of the stone.

In sharing with William one day, I remarked how ironic that even though he cannot swim he was the one who had taken me to shore and rescued me from the emotional whirlpool in which I was trapped. I felt that this time, instead of turning for him to put his arms around me, I had reached out and put my arms around him. A few days later, though, I looked again and realized that neither my husband nor anyone else had rescued me from this struggle, that I was the one who had done this myself.

I do not in any way underestimate anything that anyone did for me during this search, for there were many times I reached out, turned to, and leaned heavily on these others when I was not able to stand alone; but there is no doubt that I did this myself, and that was the way it had to be.

I have recognized that I did the most important part when I would not accept defeat nor did I sit around and whine of what life had given me. I made and followed through on my decision to seek the release from that pain which was so intense in my life.

I have been blessed with very special people to whom I was able to turn in this journey. Everyone in their own time and way sometimes held me softly and tenderly and even at times pushed me to face things I wanted to continue to avoid, always sharing with me their own strength which I needed to survive. And three wonderful men especially gave to me each from his own uniqueness, carrying, leading, following, standing beside and supporting as my needs required. No single one of my sojourners could give me everything I needed, but together they gave me all I required as each gave me something of themselves while the pain washed away, healing my heart and my soul.

But the one thing no one else could do for me was this: I had to face life for myself. AND I DID IT! I took the abilities and capabilities which are mine and used them to move forward and beyond that which was blocking my vision of the simple profoundness of life.

Daddy had frequently told us girls that *the road to hell is paved with good intentions.* How very correct he was in that. I now realize that I constructed my own highway to hell and that I was riding on it in the immediate now, not having to wait for the future of the hereafter.

I can't save the world; only myself. While I may have the knowledge and ability to help, I must also at the same time have the wisdom and compassion to allow others to live life

95

as each chooses, not to try to impose my thoughts and ideas unless others seek such from me.

Anger was my final and heaviest stone. With an anger unrecognized by myself, I was angry with the whole world. Thinking I was doing the right thing in trying to help, I was instead imposing my ways upon others. I knew how to do things and do them right. I had the answers. I could do it all if only they would listen, cooperate, and follow my lead.

But I just couldn't get these people around me to see that I knew what was best. Occasionally someone would follow my lead and prove to me that I was on the right track, but the frustration caused by those who didn't was driving me crazy.

I had turned loose of much in this travel, but anger was still holding me down and with its discovery I did some painful soul searching and personal inventory; then, with many tears I let it softly slip away from my heart.

Finally, at long last, the final step. That's the secret, if there is one: the letting go.

Yes, with the knowledge and wisdom gained through the influence of William, I found the simplicity.

On this journey I frequently stopped at the rest stations along the way to throw out clutter and garbage, for I found that none of the leftovers from the experiences in my life were recyclable. These were the complications which I had created and I was the one who needed to simplify. All the leftovers are for disposal only.

When I finally turned loose of the past I then found richness and fullness. Letting go of yesterday finally gave me the freedom to find all the wonders of today and all it has to offer.

I don't know what tomorrow may bring; in fact, there may be no tomorrow for me. I don't need tomorrow. I'm thankful for the life I'm living today. There is no guarantee as to the circumstances of my birth and death, but I'm sure going to enjoy all my todays in between.

THIS THING CALLED PRAYER

We are not puppets. God is not a giant puppeteer sitting up in heaven to jerk us around on a string. He gives us free will and expects us to exercise the choices.

I praise God. I thank God. But I don't expect to sit down and blindly wait for Him to do what I might ask of Him. He gave me abilities and capabilities and I should have the good sense to use them. Once again, it's that simple. He's not what I would make of Him.

What I found through this search has resulted in a renewal of my faith, that which was lost somewhere along the way. I fought it! I didn't want it! I didn't want this to be! Yet, this, too, I couldn't control. When I finally let go, God took over and filled my life once again.

My life was like a river as it moved at times quietly through sunshine and shadows, sometimes swiftly over rocks and through the rapids, but always forward until it has now arrived at the peaceful waters and is as the depth and width and breadth of the ocean.

God has given directions of what He expects of me in the
Ten Commandments.

The Lord's Prayer is what I ask of God.

Could it be more simple than that?

Prayer is an attitude which can be used to ignite motivation, but attitude without supporting behavior is useless. I
often wonder about the effectiveness of the monks who are
sequestered within confines of the monastery. The solitude
and quiet meditation and prayer they experience may un-
doubtedly be fulfilling to them as individuals, but their making of bread and experimentation in botany are the real rewards and achievements of this lifestyle.

I never doubted God's love for me, it is only this thing
called prayer that gives me questions. I have a problem with
prayer because I feel it is used as a shield for hiding. When
Beverly called regarding Linda's situation she said to me,
"There's not anything I can do about it. I'm going to pray for
her and go to bed."

How about the parishioner who calls the church office
and says, "I've got this problem and I want you to pray for
me," then sits down and does nothing other than whine?
Maybe that's a good time for eating. Feed your self-pity. Do
you want some cheese with your whine?

I detest self-pity and think it is the most destructive emotion in the world. I knew I was above such as this, condemn-
ing others who exhibited it; yet, I finally had to recognize
and deal with the fact that I, too, was enjoying my share of
self-pity. Say something to hurt my feelings and I would turn,
in tears, to food. Do something I could even interpret as
hurting my feelings, and I would run, in tears, to food. Come
to think of it, it's a wonder I didn't choke to death as I pushed
the food into my mouth while I was weeping.

I would eat until I was lethargic. Mine was not alcohol.
Mine was not drugs. Mine was food. Massive amounts of
food to dull the pain. I was an emotional cripple and food

was my crutch. I couldn't handle the guilt of imperfection so I would eat until my senses would finally be dulled, but even then the pain never completely went away. It was a vicious cycle. Hurt, anger, guilt, self-pity, whatever emotion the moment produced, then more food. The fat was as a neon sign to my self image as to the rest of the world, flashing *I'M FAT, I'M NOT PERFECT*.

EXCUSES

Even with all the music I care for so much, there are two particular songs I simply don't like because both are filled with excuses. The music in these is beautiful and the artists are outstanding. I'm not about to say anything against any of the people involved in these songs for each and every one is of great talent and both songs have reached the top of the music charts. It's just that I don't like constant excuses in life, and that's what's coming from these lyrics.

One of the artists sings that he could have written a book or a play or a song, or done other great things but he just couldn't do anything because he was too busy being in love; then another tells of how sometime later someone would have been ready to say something important or brought gifts or done other things with someone, but even though it's too late at least it's now being told.

Could have, would have, should have! It all hides behind excuses.

If we're going to succeed, we have to come from behind the excuses and just do it. Give me a reason, but don't give me an excuse!

Remember Garth Brooks and *The Dance*? John Michael Montgomery agrees and confirms my belief when he sings:

Life's a dance you learn as you go,
Sometimes you lead, Sometimes you follow
Don't worry 'bout what you don't know
Life's a dance you learn as you go.
There's a time to listen, A time to talk,
And you might have to crawl even after you walk
Life's a dance you learn as you go.

I'm convinced that life is like a roll of the dice. What comes up is what we get. Life doesn't single anyone out for anything good or bad. It just happens, and sometimes we get something because we are at the right place at the right time. Very important also to that fact is that if we're lucky enough to be at that place at that time, we better be prepared for what could be ours for the taking. I have no doubts, either, that we can be master of our own fate, that we can make things happen for ourselves.

When I returned to classes for computer training there was a woman in class with me who was overwhelmed with my typing speed of more than a hundred words per minute; her's was less than twenty-five words per minute. As I typed, she watched, telling herself and others in the classroom that she could master the keyboard and increase her typing speed by watching me type.

Being an attractive, well-dressed, personable woman, she fit the corporate image which the school stressed we were to achieve if we would be successful in the business world. We were all astounded to learn when she didn't report for class one week that she had applied and been hired as a computer operator by IBM. Three days later she returned to the class-room.

Her rendition of the two days she spent on the payroll at IBM was that as she sat at the computer keyboard one of the members of management walked by her position, observed her attempts at the keyboard, asked if she could type, waited for her answer, then walked away. A few minutes later she was summoned to the personnel department and terminated from employment there.

Life may not be all luck, but it seems to be luckier for those who are prepared than for those who are not.

During the months I was attending school I worked part-time hours at Delta Air Lines and it was one of the great events of my life to be hired there, and to be welcomed as a member of the Delta family. As far as I am concerned, that's first place and all the other jobs are the consolation prizes.

I don't believe there is such a thing as making a fool of one's self. If we're flexing ourselves, pushing to move beyond, that's growth. Who's to say if it's right or wrong when we dare to take a chance on life. So what if the end result is not what we wanted or expected. My friend, Janette, says that experience is what we gain when we didn't get what we wanted. Sometimes our glory lies in the trying and not in the end result. If I have to be remorseful for anything in my life, I would rather it be for something I've done rather than for something I didn't do. I know that all I'll ever get from life is that which I am willing to accept or for which I am willing to settle. I don't want to live my life in a rut of sameness day after day, and the only way I'll not do that is to try.

STEP BY STEP

*W*hen Kevin had first signed the papers to join the Marines, he was carrying his football weight and entry into the Marines required that he lose this. During the weeks between his initial join-up and the time he departed for Parris Island he had already taken off thirty pounds of weight and in his three months on the island he accomplished an additional weight loss of forty-five pounds.

Being aware of this weight loss that Kevin had experienced during his stay at that exclusive, members-only resort on the island off the coast of South Carolina, more commonly known as the United States Marine Corps basic training, I was very much aware that the exercise program he had enjoyed there had certainly contributed to his physical well-being. With that in mind, I decided that I was going to be compelled to get some regular physical activity into my life.

When I began the serious appraisal of my weight loss efforts I coupled walking with the curtailed food intake in an effort to enhance my weight loss. Walking fit both my budget and my schedule. In fact, I began walking at work. With two fifteen-minute breaks and a thirty-minute lunch break daily, I was immediately provided five hours per week for exercise.

When I first began the walking, I was hard pushed to walk five hundred yards on a fifteen minute break and I would be out of breath before I had managed even half of this distance.

However, there was never a moment of doubt in my mind that I was going to walk that full fifteen minutes twice per shift and additional thirty minute lunch break. So, my initial phase of walking was strictly for endurance. My motivation was already walking side-by-side with me from that very first step and it has never left me even for one instant. Day after day, week after week, I made that walk. As the endurance increased, I began to add distance. Sometimes that was only one added step per day, but I pushed myself continually until I was finally walking several miles daily. What about eating, you ask. Well, that simply didn't enter my mind. Remember, food was no longer the most important part of my life.

And every day that I walked while at work I never failed to stop by the scales frequented by flight attendants to check my daily weight loss. Unlike those who chose to ignore the scales, I used that as my meter of success and I *wanted* to see that gauge as the pounds dropped on an almost daily basis.

The surgeries and complications I experienced slowed me down for a while, but only for a short while. How absolutely wonderful that the direction from the doctor's office after the second surgery was that I needed to walk to build up my strength. His instructions were that I should be able to walk one mile a month after the surgery. One week following that second surgery, leaning on the arm of my husband, I walked almost five hundred feet in thirty minutes from the house towards the lake and back. One week later I walked one mile and the one month following the surgery I walked seven miles. No, that wasn't easy; and, yes, I had to push hard to accomplish these miles. The blessed people who took turns and walked these steps with me, how wonderful to have had each and everyone of them by my side. Taking turns, my husband, my sons, and my friend, Janette. No matter which of these was with me, we were always accompanied by my silent partner known as motivation.

After I had again regained the distance following surgery, I began to research techniques for getting the most from my walking, since I was still unable to get into any more of an exercise program due to my recuperation. Once again I just had to make a commitment and be consistent. What I wanted was to get the most benefit from my walking for it was pretty obvious that this was the only exercise I would be doing for quite a while. What I found and began to practice was really pretty simple, and I still continue this routine daily.

By the way, even today my motivation still continues to walk with me every step I take and there is no doubt in my mind that with this motivation ever before me I will success-fully maintain my weight loss.

Growing up in the country, seemingly always running, jumping rope, bicycle riding, or just walking though the woods helped keep my weight around normal until the time I entered high school, then the pounds began to pick up and hang onto me.

The hours in high school were more sedentary with less exercise and I also found expanded opportunities for junk food which I hadn't even known existed. At my high school graduation I weighed one hundred sixty five pounds.

Entering the work force as a secretary provided even more sedentary activity and, of course, more opportunities for un-needed calorie consumption.

Only a couple of years beyond my high school gradua-tion, John F. Kennedy became President of the United States and he encouraged physical fitness. Under his leadership and through his example, America became aware of the need for exercise. I recall the disbelief I felt when he suggested it be the goal of every American to walk fifty miles. Who in the world could ever do that, I wondered. How amazing to find after all these years that which I wouldn't even consider before as a lifetime event I now accomplish on a weekly basis.

This time, too, was the advent of health spas. Like friends and coworkers, I purchased an overpriced membership and occasionally participated, putting forth enough physical exercise spasmodically to keep my weight around the one hundred and ninety pounds to which it had now crept. Even today I find that the spa tends to be more of a social event than primarily an exercising time and I still prefer to get outside and walk whenever possible. The local shopping mall lends itself for a good walk indoors in inclement weather and management will even provide information of the required number of laps needed to accomplish a certain mileage.

I also prefer to keep the majority of my walking to myself. When I'm walking with someone else there's too much temptation and tendency to slow down and talk rather than expend maximum energy to walk, and I don't want this to be another failure in my life. Being alone while walking is also a good time to get the cobwebs out of my mind.

During employment prior to my marriage, several of us girls from the office in the state capitol building would daily walk the equivalent of a couple of miles at lunchtime. The exercise of walking and the distance covered was very good, but our destination was horribly fattening. And I wonder that these daily walks in our spike high heels may be the reason for the flat shoes we usually are now wearing!

Our daily lunches were in the *Magnolia Room* at Rich's Department Store in downtown Atlanta, where we would always completely consume the generous entree, accompanying french fries, and salad drowning in dressing, then end with a dessert of the house specialty, which was a *caramel nut ball*.

Were we even close to breaking even? How much walking is required to burn off the calories of two scoops of french vanilla ice cream covered with creamy smooth hot caramel, topped with true whipped cream, generously sprinkled with chopped Georgia pecans and finally topped with a cherry? We had, naturally, begun our workday with breakfast from the cafeteria, which consisted of several, fresh made, melt-in-your-mouth donuts of every imaginable flavor. But to cut calories we did, at least, drink the Coca-Cola product, Tab, which was new on the market.

Smoothing The Rough Edges

My sister and my mother recovered from the ordeals they encountered. These were harrowing experiences for both of them because a trust was violated through negligence, and we all learned some unforgettable lessons in life through these events. Each has her own choice to either continue or discontinue dependence upon prescription drugs. Whatever the decisions, at least they are not at crisis point and I no longer feel compelled to be the constant caretaker.

In my continued turning loose, more than two years after he had left the office where we had worked together I opened my life and told this man with whom I had worked of the feelings I had for him. Once more I knew his understanding when he gently accepted this and I was again reminded of why he is special to me. I am blessed to know him and to have walked this pathway through life together with him for a while, and I would like to forever call him my friend.

What began as a working environment relationship evolved into friendship, then became more for me. When I couldn't find it anywhere else, I reached to him and grabbed a fistful of strength and courage which I hung onto for a very long time until I could nurture my own independence. Each time I used these seeds which I had gathered from him my own strength and courage increased until I could finally draw on these within myself.

Knowing and being associated with him caused me to again feel special about myself in a way which I had forgotten. This renewal enabled me to finally break through my self-imposed entrapment of low self-esteem; then, as the ancient Phoenix arose from the ashes, I continued to lift above painful memories from my past.

And he never knew of this positive influence which he had given to me.

This caring man gave me inspiration, comfort and support, then he was part of the nightmares which threatened to destroy me. He became an important link in the series of events which pushed me to look inward and find myself. Even though he was quite a complication to me, he was also a vital part of my growth and new-found happiness.

Some rough spots of my journey have taken toll on both of us and there may even be structural damage to our foundation. He's now the engineer of this relationship and must assess and determine if we can be repaired. I can invite him to remain an active part of my life but I have to acknowledge the choice is his and allow him to make his own decision about my invitation. Another lesson I've learned is that while I can invite others into my life, they accept or deny the invitation as they so choose; by the same measure, so do I. Whether or not I ever see him again, as he said, we will always be a part of each other's life.

As I continued to look at the reality of this relationship, I found, mixed in among all the other emotions, deep feelings of guilt in myself about having unwillingly used him in my recovery. I can now accept this was permissible. He came into my life as a role model and I learned from his example. I drew from his reservoir, sifted through all I found there and retained that which I needed. I used, I did not abuse.

In my daily travels through life I am constantly in and out of the presence of others and we continually give to and draw from each other, each of us learning by example, yet always limited to giving and taking that which we have, for we can never give that which we do not have either materially, physically, spiritually, or emotionally. We take, we accept, we give, we learn, and the student eventually becomes the teacher.

Now, beyond everything, I am no longer dependent upon anyone else for emotional support. I've matured emotionally and the little girl which was within me is finally gone. At long last I've grown up and no longer do I look to others for constant approval, understanding and acceptance. That's now coming from within myself, and I like that!

If Kirby had put forth more effort perhaps he might have been able to remain on the island and become a Marine, perhaps not. We'll never know, but what we do know without a doubt is that he is now doing very well for himself. Rather like a thoroughbred race horse who sometimes makes some false beginnings out of the starting gate, Kirby has now set his sights straight ahead and is pacing himself for the race. No *place* or *show* for him, he's going to be in the winner's circle.

Classroom education continues to be a struggle for Kirby; but here's this young man who, because of learning disabilities, was unsuccessful in learning to read until age nine, now looking forward to pursuing a degree in English Literature.

From that tender, young age when he finally was able to conquer the confusion of the printed word, he has had an insatiable hunger for books. Those classics usually assigned in college classrooms as required reading have already been mastered by Kirby since these are the books he picks up and reads for leisure enjoyment.

When Kirby was doing the things necessary to graduate from high school early in order to go to the Marines he had to attend a summer school session away from his school of enrollment and had the good fortune to have as his teacher a woman who was committed to teaching her students rather than using that time for extra income with as little effort as possible on both the part of herself and her students. Daily, she assigned the students to creative writing. Kirby found his niche then and there and shows a wonderful ability for creative writing which he hopes to integrate into this degree. The beginnings of his personal library collection are such as to be envied by any collector. It is his desire and plans to attend a private college in another state (in fact, very close to the origins of his maternal grandparents) which offers an outstanding program in his course of study and interests.

Irregardless of where he is headed in the future, Kirby is happy with himself today.

Kirby is also one of a small select group of outstanding individuals. At a small table set up in the front hall of a school house, he registered to join the Cub Scouts program the same day he registered for the first grade. He continually participated in the scouting program thereafter and, at age eighteen, was one of the less than two percent of scouts to earn the rank of Eagle in the program of the Boy Scouts of America.

Kirby experienced the loss of a special friend, Sammie Henderson, when she died in an automobile crash as she was driving home from work during an early morning hour in March of 1993. He has deep pain and I ache for him as he faces this loss. Because of what I lived and learned through the death of my sister can I now truly empathize with my son as he also looks inward to confront his own grief.

In parenting our sons, while having specific expectations of them insofar as integrity and moral development, we likewise allowed much leniency and freedom, encouraging them to make their own decisions whenever possible, giving them guidance and direction, reminding them to always consider each decision made, knowing they would have to live with the consequences of any action taken.

Thus, when Kevin decided to quit school prior to graduation and join the Marines, we backed him in his decision. Who is to say that was a right or wrong decision. We can all look at the road not taken in life and live with *what-if's*.

Through the Marines, Kevin has successfully entered a field of training with a career potential which will allow him a most comfortable life in the years to come. Everyone who knows Kevin says he was born to be a Marine; in fact, he's taken to it like a duck to water and it seems that he's Marine to the marrow of his bones. The discipline and experiences he has encountered certainly single him out as one of the chosen few.

As an avionics technician, Kevin gets hands-on experience in taking apart and putting together, this time on aircraft. He definitely trained for that aspect for years. Anything and everything, indoors or out. Clocks, watches, video games, radios, televisions, toasters, blenders, and all parts of his yellow Volkswagen, including but not limited to the motor. Nothing missed his scrutiny. If it had a moving part, he wanted to know how it worked. He and his daddy would frequent trashpiles along the side of the roadway looking for anything that even resembled a motor, just so he could take it apart. Nothing was beyond his imagination and desire for knowledge.

This was all well and good except for the time, around age twelve, he decided for some reason to disassemble his bicycle. The weather wasn't particularly such as to prevent the work outdoors, but Kevin did this in his room in the middle of his bed. Knowing that he was going to probably catch some kind of flack if he dared to do these mechanics on the bed covers, he removed bed spread, blankets, sheets, and mattress cover and then placed the bicycle, part by part, black grease and all, directly on the mattress.

If Kevin gets any ideas such as this while serving his time in those Marine barracks, I just hope that Master Gunnery Sergeant is as lenient and understanding as Kevin's parents were in that particular instance in his youth!

These two young men. My sons. Each stands and walks tall in life. Both are of good character and high morals. Blessed am I to be their mother.

My husband continues to work too hard and too many hours and we still don't yet see the light at the end of the tunnel for our financial situation.

We learned how to cut corners financially and found, for instance, that we could survive with one automobile between us rather than the expense of operating two. That's a wonderful experience, for it gives us more time together and who could ask for anything greater than personalized service with door-to-door pickup and delivery by my chauffeur.

We've managed to hold onto our home so far even though there still may be a *For Sale* sign in the front yard. If that happens, whether by necessity or by choice, we'll deal with it when the time comes. Whatever happens about the house, we can always look forward to the enjoyment of many hours in the air using our Delta flight privileges, and we'll do that at every opportunity! If we're successful in keeping the house, we'll eventually spend evenings sitting in the swing in the backyard while watching the sun set across the lake.

After our marriage ceremony those many years ago, William and I honeymooned in Nassau. We are now planning and looking forward to the celebration of our twenty-fifth wedding anniversary, when we are going to return to the Bahamas for a second honeymoon.

We thank Mr. Vince Gill for giving us a song which so beautifully presents and celebrates our continuing love and caring for each other, when he sings:

Look at us, after all these years together
Look at us, after all we've been through
Look at us, still leaning on each other
If you want to see how true love can be
Then just look at us

And he then sums it up very well when he sings,

In a hundred years from now I know without a doubt
They'll all look back at us and wonder how we
made it all work out.

Our experiences certainly have not been unique in the job loss and its repercussions and we have found support as well as understanding from friends, neighbors, and coworkers who have also suffered loss of employment themselves.

And let no one underestimate the price extracted from our society by unemployment, both emotionally and financially. The percentages as reported by the media on a monthly basis are only facts and figures and may seem insignificantly small. However, these are human lives which are dependent upon employment for survival; and unemployment is a personal pain.

Sadly, my sister is gone and nothing can change nor replace that loss for me. I shall always miss her love of life and compassionate understanding, ready smile and laughter, joy and happiness, and her role in my life.

In dealing with Barbara's death and the other trauma I experienced during this period I most likely could have been a thesis for a degree in psychiatry. I looked inward, faced myself and experienced more than I could have even begun

117

to expect, and sometimes the pain of turning loose was even greater than that which I had initially experienced.

There is yet one anger within me which I do not antici-pate will leave, and that is my anger about cancer. I am angry that cancer took my sister away from me. I am angry that I have to bury my friends with whom I should be able to share the golden years, men and women in their twenties and thir-ties and forties and fifties who are destroyed by cancer in their prime of life. Angry that cancer takes the children and denies them a full life. Angry that cancer takes our older generation who should be here to lead us. I am angry at the pain and suffering and devastation caused by cancer even to those who survive its attack.

Yes, I am angry about cancer and that so much funding in the name of research is not yielding the cure. I'm angry, too, that there are not public demonstrations against cancer and that so few high–profile people are demanding action or draw-ing attention to this disease and its victims.

Why doesn't demand for minutely extensive research and cure for the unpreventable cancer get as much attention as the preventable pregnancy which ends in abortion and the likewise preventable tragedy of AIDS?

Have we become so complacent as a society that we will simply accept death by cancer without a forceful public out-cry?

Yes, I continue to be angry at cancer and want to see it annilated as surely as the destruction it permeates.

THE NEXT STEP

his book evolved from my search for release from a pain which reached into the depths of my being. In this search I found I was not alone, that I walked with others along this pathway of incredible pain. When my search finally ended I had realized that beneath this pain lies an equally incredible happiness.

For you who are yet searching, with all my heart I encourage you to continue to seek until you, too, find the answers in your life which result in the peace which is there just for the accepting.

The experiences of my life wrote this book, one word at a time, each then being compounded into sentences, paragraphs, pages, and chapters. Life, likewise, finally gave me the final steps of this part of my journey the same as in the past, always in a suspiciously unexpected way as to time and circumstance. Behold now the beauty and glory and peace within me.

The final chapter of my life is yet to come; only with my death will my journey be fully completed. When that time comes, please don't send flowers! Until that moment I have my todays and miles to go. Some of these will be with my husband and, yes, many times we'll even be hand–in–hand; there will be pathways traveled with my sons and also in shared friendship with some special people in my life, and there will be times when I will be alone.

I expect there will be both laughter and tears along the way, but the best difference now is that I don't have to always have someone along to hold my hand. I can now do it alone. I no longer feel the need for constant approval; I can accept disapproval and survive without guilt. That simply doesn't matter anymore because I don't have to strive for perfection by anyone's standards.

When I began this search it never entered my mind that I would find this release from food, this new me, and this much freedom and happiness in my life. I was only looking to survive, and in the process I found how to live. In the simplicity, with the complications gone, I am now living from the inside out rather than from the outside in.

My soul had been torn open to expose incredible pain. By dealing with this pain and allowing the healing, I was taken from a life of mediocrity to unmatched richness and fullness. I discovered that incredible happiness lies just beneath the surface of daily living, faintly concealed and hidden by the pain and is waiting there to erupt into life just as a volcano throws forth its contents in brilliance. Even in daily walks through life the surface is often scratched and short bursts of happiness bubble forth, but never to the fullness of the complete happiness which is there just for the taking. The only requirement is to turn loose of the other debris in life which prevents me from reaching out and accepting this completeness.

Are you ready to give up control in your life? Keep testing life, asking questions, seeking answers. Keep searching; but always remember you have to accept the answers that come, you cannot force the answers you want. That's controlling, and it won't work.

Consider the jigsaw puzzle. It has to be put together piece by piece, and it only comes out right when the pieces are fit together as intended. The pieces that don't fit cannot be forced.

Turn loose. Begin your flight. Rise up and fly free. As you ascend and look down on your life, things which are of such greatness at this point will become smaller and smaller and of less importance in the panoramic view from greater heights.

Wherever your journey takes you, always know you are not alone in your travels. I'm pulling for you and the successful completion of your search. I want success for you as much as you want it for yourself.

The trip will have its rough spots, but don't give up. That's where motivation comes in and why it is so important.

Know, too, that another reward of finding yourself is that you'll salvage your self-esteem and find there is always hope. You will also be filled with happiness which comes from being at peace with yourself, and that will be worth all the effort you ever have to put forward.

…and Alice wondered:

"Who in the world am I? Ah, that's the great puzzle!"

EPILOGUE

*I*t has been almost two years since I began recording this manuscript, while both visible and invisible changes have taken place for me. These changes, which still occur daily as I reach for greater distances in my personal life, range from the minute to the absolute grand slam; and there's still even more room for the continued growth which I reach to accomplish. One of the most enjoyable experiences for me has been in following the career of Collin Raye. I'd like to consider myself his Number One fan; but if I can't claim that status, at least I'm in the Top Ten! I travel both short and great distances to attend his concerts at every opportunity.

It is great pleasure for me to personally give him bouquets of flowers as tokens of admiration, to give and take back simple exchanges of special feelings between an artist and one who recognizes and enjoys the gift of his music, and to simply listen to the songs he performs.

His most recently released album entitled EXTREMES ca-
resses every human emotion. As I listen to these selections, I
alternately smile or laugh aloud or maybe even quietly hum
or sing along with him. Some of the songs urge me to dance
around the room as he lends his voice to the spirits which
stir to the depths of my feelings. Then there are those lyrics
which reach down to touch and lift my tears to the surface as
I feel and empathize with the human souls which have a part
in these productions, from the writers through the perform-
ers to the listeners.

From the menu offered in this collection, I have discovered yet one more song which will become another indelible
part of me; one which I feel sums up all I have tried to record
in this book, what I would hold out to every person who
reads these pages. For myself, I like to interpret the *me* in
this song as *life* itself!

To you who are looking for your own answers, I would
challenge you to continue your journey; keeping in mind as
you chart your course the words penned by Chris Farren and
John Hobbs in their song IF I WERE YOU.

You wanna know
Where we go from here
So many roads
But none that seem clear
Is what we have enough
To last a whole life through
Who knows, who knows.

So you're asking me
What do we do
Cuz time moves so fast
And the chances seem so few
Is it too much to think
That we could have it all
Who knows, we may never know

But if I were you I'd promise to
Live life for all it's worth
Take all that you've been given
And leave your mark upon this earth
Trust your heart to tell you
Everything you'll ever need
And if I were you
I'd fall in love with me

So hold me close
I'll kiss away your fears
I won't promise the moon
But I promise to be here
And what if together
It gets better every day
Who knows, who knows

But if I were you I'd promise to
Live life for all it's worth
Take all that you've been given
And leave your mark upon this earth
Trust your heart to tell you
Everything you'll ever need
And if I were you
I'd fall in love with me

The autobiographical story told in this book is not about losing; rather, it is about winning.

In dealing with significant personal trauma, I journeyed inward to find and confront the cause of intense emotional pain in my life. In this search I found many clues, ultimately realizing I was feeding a self-imposed guilt. Somewhere along the way I had assumed perfection was required of me. Knowing I was falling short of that achievement, I used food to assuage my terrible feeling of failure. Excessive food was as a drug to me. I would eat until I was lethargic and the resulting dullness would take off the edge of my pain; yet, even though the pain would be somewhat softened, I remained constantly aware of its presence.

Exposing and examining life's pathway helped me to discover that my overeating was closely related to residual pains that had long been eating at me. Honest self-examination helped me to turn loose of the chronic hurt and allow healing. The resulting release of both undesirable pain and weight was thus accomplished.

Through a process of honest self-evaluation I shed my tattered wings of perfection, discarded the burden of my baggage of guilt, and let go of trying to control the circumstances of life—for myself and others. Through that process I found happiness beyond imagination.

As I focused on reality, I finally accepted responsibility for myself which gave me the freedom to finally just be me and to know that's all I ever needed to be! This enabled me to accept and love myself, then to reach out to also embrace and allow others back into my life—thus casting off a self-imposed emotional isolation.

Once I realized it is never too late to be all I ever could have been, I resolved to use the inner resources of strength and courage which I found to set and reach that goal for myself. Losing weight was the bonus for my efforts of self-examination...and I'll take that reward any day!!!

Rather than remaining trapped or short-circuited by the past, I have chosen to accept life as the adventure it is. When I open my eyes daily from restful sleep, I am awakened by an inner excitement as I look forward to today's surprises in this journey through life.

I now have the desire and dedication to rise above being insecure and overweight and to share my experiences with others who likewise face the concealed pain which results in obesity. It is my desire to instill hope, trusting there is encouragement in my story to inspire you to reach for your own happiness.

As you progress in your journey, I wish for you

PEACE, JOY, LOVE & LAUGHTER

SUGGESTED READING

Jonathan Livingston Seagull
 —Richard Bach
  with photographs by Russell Munson
When Life Throws You A Curveball, Hit It
 —Criswell Freeman
Full Lives
Women Who Have Freed Themselves From Food & Weight Obsession
 —Lindsey Hall
Adult Children: The Secrets of Dysfunctional Families
 —John Friel and Linda Friel
Women Who Run With the Wolves
 —Clarissa Pinhola Estes
Gift From The Sea
 —Anne Morrow Lindbergh
It's Not What You Eat, It's What's Eating You
 —Janet Greeson
The Celestine Prophecy
 —James Redfield
The Power of Positive Living
The Power of Positive Thinking
 —Norman Vincent Peale
Healing Your Insecurities
 —Roy Hicks
Healing of Emotions
 —Chris Griscom
Seven Habits of Highly Effective People
 —Stephen Covey
Self-Love
 —Dr. Robert H. Schuller
Alcoholics Anonymous
 —The Big Book and *The Twelve Steps*
Codependents' Guide to The Twelve Steps
 —Melody Beattie
What You Feel You Can Heal
Men Are From Mars, Women Are From Venus
 —John Gray